116

Riel Mini-Conference Papers

Louis Riel
& the Métis

A. S. Lussier,
Editor

ISBN 0-919143-16-4

iii

Third Printing 1998

 **PEMMICAN PUBLICATIONS INC.**

Unit 2-1635 Burrows Avenue / Winnipeg, Manitoba, Canada / R2X 3B5

i v

v

Dedicated to:
Professor Vic Batzel
Professor Peter Brown
Mrs. Colette Brown
for their encouragement
and help in my study
of Métis history.

About the Authors

Ken Hatt: Member of the Sociology-Anthropology Department, Carlton University, Ottawa, Ontario.

Gilles Martel: Sociologist from l'Université de Sherbrooke, Sherbrooke, Québec. He is also co-author of *Louis Riel: Poésies de jeunesse* - Editions du Blé, St. Boniface, Manitoba, 1977.

Thomas E. Flanagan: Member of the Department of Political Science, University of Calgary. Dr. Flanagan has written extensively on Riel's messianic vision. He also co-authored *Louis Riel: Poésies de jeunesse.*

Fritz Pannekoek: Chief of the Historical Research Section, Parks Canada, Prairie Region, presently working on the Social History of the Fur Trade.

John Foster: Member of the History Department, University of Alberta, Edmonton, Alberta.

Raymond Huel: Member of the History Department, University of Lethbridge. Raymond has done most of his research in the areas of the French-Canadian fact in Saskatchewan as well as the French-Catholics of Western Canada.

Glen Campbell: Member of the Department of Romance Studies, University of Calgary. He co-authored *Louis Riel: Poésies de jeunesse.*

Contents

Introduction   11
Antoine S. Lussier

The Riel Project   15
Dr. G. F. G. Stanley

Le Projet Riel   18
Dr. G. F. G. Stanley

1. Louis Riel as Charismatic Leader   23
   Ken Hatt

2. Les Indiens dans la pensée
   messianique de Louis Riel   31
   Gilles Martel

3. Louis Riel's Name "David"   55
   Thomas Flanagan

4. Some Comments on the Social Origins
   of the Riel Protest of 1869   65
   Fritz Pannekoek

5. The Métis: The People and the Term   77
   John Foster

6. Louis Schmidt: A Forgotten Métis   87
   Raymond Huel

7. A Survey of Louis Riel's Poetry   95
   Glen Campbell

8. The Political Thought of Louis Riel   111
   Thomas Flanagan

Appendix
Louis Riel: A Preliminary
Bibliography, 1963-1978   129
   Thérèse D. Lafontaine

Footnotes   163

Introduction

NO NAME in Western Canadian history has created so much emotional debate as that of Louis Riel. Perceived as a traitor by some Canadians, as a martyr by others, the man continues to be an enigma to Canadian historians. The papers in this edition illustrate this very well.

This volume contains a majority of papers read at a Louis Riel Conference held at the University of Alberta, Edmonton, on October 21, 1978, under the sponsorship of the Riel Project. Included are papers that are being published for the first time.

A recent study of Riel by Tom Flanagan entitled *Louis "David" Riel* has shed new light on the Métis leader. Breaking from the traditional view of Riel expressed in G.F.G. Stanley's biography *Louis Riel,* Flanagan looked at the messianic motives of Riel instead of the traditional martyr-traitor analysis that has been given much credence in Métis historiography. Following in Flanagan's footsteps is an article by Ken Hatt entitled "Louis Riel as Charismatic Leader". Hatt explores the reasons why Riel was able to dominate a skeptical Métis populace with charismatic leadership. Hatt argues that even though Riel had little support among the Métis he was able to manipulate them in attempting to fulfill his own messianic dreams. Using Max Weber's "Configurational Model of Charisma," Hatt presents a potent argument for additional research on Riel as the leader of a "leading faction in a larger agrarian protest."

Though little has been written about the role of the Indians in the 1869-70 Rebellion at Red River, such is not the case in 1885. Unfortunately, historians have tended to emphasize the roles of Big Bear, Crowfoot, Wandering Spirit and Poundmaker as either pacifists or activists during the events of 1885. How Riel viewed the Indian role in the conflict has been demonstrated by G.F.G. Stanley in *The Birth of Western Canada* and Desmond Morton in *The Last War Drum.* But the Indian in Riel's "New World" and, the importance he attached to Indian ancestry regarding Métis "Native Claims" have as yet to be

11

adequately researched. Gilles Martel's "Les Indiens dans la pensée messianique de Louis Riel" is a pioneering effort in attempting to understand what emphasis Riel placed on Indian ancestry for the Métis. According to Martel, Riel
never suggested that the Métis return to an Indian lifestyle but "le sang indien
. . . assure aux Métis un droit inaliénable à la possession du sol de la nouvelle
Terre Promise." Martel's article is also effective in demonstrating Riel's
obsession with geneology, especially in his attempt to define the mission of his
chosen people. Here Riel rejects the "Ten Lost Tribes of Israel" thesis and
argues for the French-Catholic mission. The Indians then are to become just
another of the many nations Riel foresaw living in his "New World."

"Louis Riel's Name 'David' " by Tom Flanagan explores Riel's search for
"a symbolic explanation of his own life and the history of his people." Riel
continuously drew parallels between his life and that of David. With the sense
of mission that obsessed him, Riel even went as far as to compare the plight of
the Métis with that of the Hebrews in the *Old Testament*. Since the Hebrews
and the Métis both had been persecuted and David and Riel made themselves
the martyrs of their respective causes, Riel could not help but make "David's
career the model of his own." This article is most intriguing because Flanagan
argues that Riel used the *Bible* as his force in promoting revolutionary change,
either by violence or passivity.

To date there have been as many as five interpretations given of the 1869-70
Rebellion in Manitoba, describing it as (a) a French-English conflict, (b)
civilization vs. the frontier, (c) a civil war, (d) a conspiracy of the Catholic
clergy, and (e) the decapitation theory that Sylvia Van Kirk is currently explor-
ing. In "Some Comments on the Social Origins of the Riel Protest of 1869,"
Fritz Pannekoek questions the validity of these theories which he feels have
been advanced without proper analysis of the roots of the rebellion. Pan-
nakoek urges the historian to reexamine "the social, economic and religious
background" of the resistance with the hope that new light can be shed upon
it. The questions asked in his conclusion deserve attention and consideration
for further research.

"The Métis: The People and the Term" by John Foster is a most controversial piece of literature because of the question it asks of researchers and writers
of Métis history. Foster asks what right do writers have of attributing cultural
traits and traditions to any group of people who do not identify themselves as
such? Quoting Foster: "Identifying people of mixed ancestry historically, one
must take into account their own view of themselves." This is true of today.
How does one define a Métis in contemporary times given that the term is now
synonymous with Non-Status Indians, Half-Breeds, and in some Métis
organizations, whites?

Throughout his political career, Riel had three secretaries, one of whom was
Louis Schmidt. In "Louis Schmidt: A Forgotten Métis," Raymond Huel
documents the reactions that Schmidt had with respect to Riel's leadership at

Batoche in 1885. Using sources that have been scarcely researched, Huel presents a description of Riel as seen by a person "close to the action" and a former classmate of Riel's. The article is an ideal complement to Dr. Donald Smith's work on Henry Jackson, another of Riel's secretaries.

In 1977, Professor Campbell co-authored a pioneering effort entitled *Louis Riel: Posésies de jeunesse* in which Riel's "political and religious verse as well as songs, fables and love poems," were adequately described. The paper in this volume gives further "insight and perspective" on the man and attempts to introduce another aspect of Riel to the reader.

"The Political Thought of Riel" is a discussion of Riel's main political preoccupations. According to Tom Flanagan, they were: nationalism, native rights, and the relationship of religious to secular authority. Tracing Riel's personal history and the institutional influences that affected his political positions, Flanagan attempts to explain Riel's political philosophy and why Canadians need to understand Riel's political thought.

In no way does this volume purport to be a comprehensive study and analysis of Riel or of the Métis people that he led. Rather it presents new sample studies about the Métis leader and his people. Hopefully this volume will stimulate the reader to delve more deeply into other aspects of Riel, and the Métis who believed in his "Nouvelle Nation."

A.S. Lussier, Director
Native Studies Program
15 McLean Hall
University of Saskatchewan
Saskatoon, Saskatchewan
S7N 0W0

The Riel Project

George F.G. Stanley

SEVERAL OF the papers in this volume were presented at a small academic session—advertised as the "Riel Mini-Conference"—held at the University of Alberta on October 21, 1978. This session was important as marking the double purpose. It was, first of all, a forum in which to exchange ideas about Louis Riel's significance, the Métis experience, and the causes and implications of the 1870 and 1885 uprisings. In addition to this, it provided the opportunity to inform Canadian academic historians, as well as the general public of what the Riel Project was all about.

The *raison d'être* of the Project is to collect and publish the complete writings of Louis Riel. When completed, the publication, which will be called *Louis Riel, Collected Papers, Critical Edition/Louis Riel, Ecrits complets, édition critique,* should prove of considerable value to students of Riel. In the past, such students had no choice but to spend long periods of time and money searching for and examining documents, scattered across Canada from British Columbia to New Brunswick, and in the United States from Montana to Rhode Island. In a few years, it will be feasible for the scholar to find much of what he seeks in the nearest well-stocked library. The ready availability of Riel's writings should lead directly to improvements, both qualitative and quantitative, in the secondary literature on Riel. There already exists, of course, a very respectable body of literature on Riel; but a project of this nature should encourage still further research, as well as uncover documents shedding new light on Riel's personality, the people he led, and the events in which he played a major role.

There has been a demand as well as a real need for publications of this kind in Canada. In fact, the application to the Social Sciences and Humanities Research Council of Canada was made in direct response to the specific requests of scholars. Several years ago, the Western Canadiana Publications Project (WCPP) of the University of Alberta began enquiring of scholars in Western Canada their views of what material most urgently needed to be made readily available, material which would shed light on the Western Canadian experience. The overwhelming response to this survey, was a demand for the publication of Riel's papers. It was believed that scholarship in Western Canada would be greatly enriched were Riel's writings accessible in published form. Accordingly, the WCPP, with Professors N. Parker-Jervis and D. Jackel of the English Department of the University of Alberta playing leading roles, set about putting together a team of scholars for just such a project, and making a formal application to the SSHRCC for financing. There is little point in describing in detail the process of negotiation that ensued as a result of the application, except to say that the demand for the publication of Riel's papers was reaffirmed by the scholars who were asked by the SSHRCC to submit assessments of the application.

The intent of the editors in publishing Riel's papers is to be as faithful as possible to what Riel himself wrote—faithful both in substantivals and in accidentals. The publication will thus be a "critical" edition in the sense that errors will be noted, variants recorded, and annotations furnished. In the interests of objectivity, the annotations will be written in as "neutral" a fashion as possible, serving the specific purpose of explaining Riel's reference to people, places, and events. Each of the four volumes planned will be preceded by an introduction by the editor of the volume. In my capacity as chief editor, I will write a general introduction to the series as a whole. For scholars interested in consulting the secondary literature available, there will be a thorough bibliography of the literature on Riel from the time of the Red River uprising to the present.

The Riel Project team is an inter-disciplinary one, and, we feel, happily so. The various realms of scholarship which the different members of our editorial board represent, help us to understand Riel's life and times from the broadest possible perspective, and will hopefully eliminate any possible bias that might arise from studying his writings using the methodology and the concerns of a single discipline. We have also found that the editing of a historical figure's papers poses a variety of technical problems, which require specialized knowledge from a number of different academic areas to overcome. Aside from my own role as General Editor, there are four volume editors of the project; Thomas Flanagan, a political scientist at the University of Calgary, who also acts as Deputy Editor; Glen Campbell, a Professor of Romance Languages, also at the University of Calgary; Gilles Martel, a sociologist from the Université de Sherbrooke; and, Raymond Huel, a Professor of History at the University of Lethbridge, who took the place of Robert Painchaud (University of Manitoba) when the latter was tragically killed in an accident in 1978. In addition, three associate editors will provide assistance in an advisory capacity; John Foster (History) and Roger Motut (Romance Languages) of the University of Alberta, and Douglas Lochhead (Canadian Studies) of Mount Allison University. Professor Lochhead has, unfortunately, been compelled to withdraw from the project for reasons of health. Finally, the editorial board is completed by Claude Rocan, who acts as Administrative Officer, and who is located in Edmonton.

The financing for the project is provided by a grant from the Social Sciences and Humanities Council of Canada. The sponsoring institution is the University of Alberta, while the Universities of Calgary, Sherbrooke, and Lethbridge are supporting institutions. The project will be funded over the years 1978-83, to coincide with the centennial of the 1885 North-West Rebellion.

The initial task undertaken by the editorial team is that of locating the whereabouts of the various Riel manuscripts still in existence. This done, the next step is to obtain permission to make photocopies or microfilms of these documents. The task was considerably simplified by the fact that the editors, having already done considerable research on Riel before the project was conceptualized, had accurate records of the holdings of different institutions. Based on these records, an "Inventory of Original Manuscripts of Louis Riel" was drawn up, which served as a guide in approaching different institutions, and individuals, and which will be included in the final publications. It is impossible to be certain, of course, that this inventory is exhaustive. There are conceivably public institutions which may hold documents of which we are unaware. An even more serious problem is that private individuals, still unknown to us, may possess Riel manuscripts. One of our purposes in publicizing the project as widely as possible, is to encourage such institutions or individuals, in the interests of historical truth, to make known to us any Riel documents they may possess, and to permit one or more of our editors to examine them and make copies of them.

On the basis of what has been accomplished so far, we are satisfied that our progress has been relatively smooth. Thanks largely to the generous cooperation of all the repositories with which we have corresponded, notably the Provincial Archives of Manitoba and the Public Archives of Canada—which have, by far, the largest collections of Riel documents—it is estimated that at the time of writing, over eighty percent of the items listed in our inventory have been assembled. By the autumn of 1979, it is hoped that our files will be, as far as we know, complete.

Obviously, we can never be satisfied that we have collected all of Riel's extant writings. Even though the Métis leader was careful about his papers (did he anticipate their publication?), there can be no doubt that over the years some, at least, have been destroyed or discarded by those to whom they were addressed. The most one can hope to do is to fill in the gaps as much as possible. In an effort to do this, the papers of other prominent figures of Riel's times will be searched, in order to find copies of Riel's letters which may have been transcribed by others. Riel lived, alas, prior to the advent of the photocopying machine. When the originals are unavailable, and if there is solid reason to believe in the authenticity of hand-written copies, they will be included in the publication, with mention being made of their provenance. Likewise, a search of the contemporary newspapers will also be conducted, to collect let-

ters by Riel to the editors of various newspapers, and which were published by
them.

The essays included in the present volume will help to clarify important
aspects of Riel's life and times. Riel was a complex and a controversial figure,
and each new book and article helps us to grasp more fully the goals he sought,
and the obstacles, external and internal, that beset his path. It is the sincere
hope of the members of the Riel Project, and indeed their expectation, that the
publication of Riel's papers will encourage historians, professional and
amateur alike, to contribute further to the understanding of the man who led
the Métis cause in 1869 and 1885.

Le Projet Riel

George F.G. Stanley

PLUSIEURS COMMUNICATIONS qui paraissent à l'intérieur de ce volume,
ont été présentées à une réunion académique restreinte—annoncée sous le titre
de "Mini-conférence Riel"—à l'Université de l'Alberta le 21 octobre 1978.
Cette réunion était importante parce qu'elle marquait l'inauguration officielle
du Projet Riel. La conférence, en fait, répondait à un double but. Elle offrait
tout d'abord un forum pour échanger des idées au sujet de ce que signifie
Louis Riel, ainsi que de l'expérience des Métis, et des causes et des implications
des soulèvements de 1870 et de 1885. En outre, ce forum fournissait l'occasion
d'informer les historiens des universités candiennes ainsi que le public en
général de la nature et des buts du Projet Riel.

La raison d'être du projet est la collection et la publication en entier des
écrits de Riel. Une fois terminée, cette collection qui sera intitulée *Louis Riel,
Collected Papers, Critical Edition/Louis Riel, Ecrits complets, édition critique*, devrait fournir une aide considérable aux étudiants qui s'intéressent à
Riel. Dans le passé, ces étudiants n'avaient que le choix de dépenser beaucoup
de temps et d'argent à faire de la recherche et à examiner des documents épar-
pillés à travers le Canada, de la Colombie Britannique au Nouveau Brunswick,
ainsi qu'aux Etats-Unis, de Montana à Rhode Island. Dans quelques années, il
sera possible au chercheur de trouver en grande partie ce qui l'intéresse, dans
une bibliothèque voisine et bien garnie. Cette disponibilité des écrits de Riel
devrait aussi conduire à une amélioration, autant qualitative que quantitative,

des écrits secondaires sur Riel. Un projet de cette nature devrait donc encourager davantage la recherche et faire découvrir des documents qui pourraient jeter une nouvelle lumière sur la personnalité de Riel, le peuple qu'il dirigeait et les événements dans lesquels il a joué un rôle majeur.

Il y a eu au Canada une demande ainsi qu'un réel besoin de publications de ce genre. En effet, la demande de subventions au Conseil de recherches en sciences humaines du Canada a été fait en réponse directe aux requêtes de savants. Il y a quelques années, le Western Canadiana Publications Project (WCCP) de l'Université de l'Alberta a fait une enquête auprès des savants de l'Ouest canadien pour connaître leurs idées sur le matériel dont on avait le plus besoin et qui devrait être le plus rapidement disponible, matériel qui jetterait un peu de lumière sur l'expérience de l'Ouest canadien. La très grande majorité des réponses à cette enquête a été la demande qu'on publie les écrits de Riel. On croyait que les écrits de Riel, une fois publiés et accessibles, enrichiraient grandement par le fait même, l'érudition et le savoir dans l'Ouest canadien. En conséquence, le WCCP, au sein duquel les professeurs N. Parker-Jervis et D. Jackel du Département d'Anglais de l'Université de l'Alberta jouaient un rôle prépondérant, se mit à l'oeuvre pour recruter un équipe de savants pour un tel projet et pour faire une demande de subvention au Conseil de recherches en sciences humaines du Canada. Il ne servirait à rien de décrire en détail le processus de négociations qui s'ensuivit, si ce n'est pour mentionner que cette demande de publication des écrits de Riel a de nouveau reçu l'appui de savants auxquels le CRSHC avait demandé de soumettre leur évaluation de la requête.

En publiant les écrits de Riel, l'intention des éditeurs est d'être aussi fidèle que possible à ce que Riel lui-même a écrit—fidèle quant au fond et aux accidentaux. La publication sera donc une édition "critique" en ce sens qu'on y notera les erreurs, on enregistrera les variantes et l'on fournira les annotations. Pour raisons d'objectivité, les annotations seront écrites d'une façon aussi "neutre" que possible, ne servant que le but précis d'expliquer les références faites par Riel à des personnes, des endroits ou des événements. Chacun des quatre volumes tels que planifiés sera précédé d'une introduction par l'éditeur du volume. Comme éditeur en chef, j'écrirai une introduction générale à la série.

Pour les savants qui seraient intéressés à consulter les oeuvres secondaires disponibles sur Riel, il y aura une bibliographie complète de ces écrits à partir de l'insurrection de la Rivière Rouge jusqu'au présent.

L'équipe du Projet Riel est une équipe inter-disciplinaire et nous croyons que c'est là une bonne chose. Les différents domaines de connaissance représentés par notre bureau d'éditeurs nous aident à comprendre la vie et la période de Riel sous le jour d'une perspective aussi large que possible, et nous l'espérons, permettra d'éliminer toute partialité qui pourrait ressortir de l'étude de ses écrits due aux exigences de méthodes et d'intérêts d'une seule

discipline. Nous avons aussi découvert qu'éditer les écrits d'une figure historique pose une variété de problèmes techniques qui requièrent pour les sur-
monter une connaissance spécialisée de différents domaines. En plus de mon
rôle comme éditeur général, quatre éditeurs de volumes se partagent le projet:
Thomas Flanagan, professeur en Sciences Politiques à l'Université de Calgary,
qui agit comme sous-éditeur; Glen Campbell, professeur de langues romanes,
lui aussi de l'Université de Calgary; Gilles Martel, sociologue de l'Université
de Sherbrooke; et Raymond Huel, professeur d'histoire à l'Université de
Lethbridge qui a remplacé Robert Painchaud (Université du Manitoba) lorsque celui-ci a tragiquement perdu la vie dans un accident en 1978. Trois
éditeurs adjoints aideront aussi en leur capacité d'aviseurs: John Foster
(Histoire); Roger Motut (Langues romanes) de l'Université de l'Alberta et
Douglas Lochhead (Etudes canadiennes) de l'Université Mount Allison.
Malheureusement, le professeur Lochhead a dû se retirer du projet pour
raisons de santé. Enfin, le Bureau des Editeurs compte aussi Claude Rocan
qui, en sa capacité de coordinateur, à ses bureaux a Edmonton. Les fonds du
Projet proviennent d'une subvention du Conseil de recherches en sciences humaines du Canada. Le projet est parrainé par l'Université de l'Alberta, tandis
que les Universités de Calgary, Sherbrooke et Lethbridge agissent comme institutions de soutien. La subvention du Projet sera répartie entre les années
1978 et 1983, et les quatre ou cinq volumes de l'édition seront publiés par les
Presses de l'Alberta en 1984-85, dates qui coïncident avec le centenaire du
soulèvement du Nord-Ouest en 1885.

La tâche initiale entreprise par l'équipe des éditeurs est celle de découvrir où
se trouvent les divers manuscrits de Riel. Ceci fait, il faudra ensuite obtenir la
permission de faire des photocopies ou des microfilms de ces documents. La
tâche s'est avérée considérablement simplifiée du fait que les éditeurs avaient
déjà fait une recherche considérable sur Riel avant la conception même du
Projet et avaient déjà en mains des dossiers exacts sur ce que possédaient les
diverses institutions. A partir de ces dossiers, un "Inventaire des manuscrits
originaux de Louis Riel" a été élaboré, lequel a servi de guide pour entrer en
communication avec diverses institutions et individus, et qui sera inclus dans la
publication finale. Il est évidement impossible d'être assuré que cet inventaire
soit complet. Il se pourrait qu'il y ait certaines institutions publiques ayant en
leur possession des documents dont nous ne connaissons pas l'existence. Un
problème encore plus grand est celui de personnes, encore inconnues de nous,
qui puissent posséder des manuscrits de Riel. Un de nos objectifs, en faisant
autant de publicité que possible autour du Projet, est précisément d'encourager ces institutions et ces personnes, dans l'intérêt de la vérité historique,
à nous faire connaître tout document de Riel en leur possession et de permettre
à un ou à quelques-uns de nos éditeurs, de les examiner et d'en faire des copies.

En nous basant sur ce qui a été accompli jusqu'ici, nous sommes satisfaits
du progrès à peu près sans heurts du Projet. Grâce à la coopération généreuse

de tout le personnel des archives avec lequel nous avons correspondu, en particulier les Archives Provinciales du Manitoba et les Archives Publiques du Canada—qui possèdent d'emblée la plus grande collection de documents sur Riel—nous estimons au moment où ces lignes sont écrites, avoir assemblé au dessus de quatre-vingt pour cent des items sur la liste de notre inventairre. Vers l'automne de 1979, d'après nos connaissances actuelles, nous espérons avoir complété nos dossiers.

Bien entendu, nous ne serons jamais assurés d'avoir collectionné tous les écrits de Riel qui existent encore. Même si le chef métis prenait grand soin de ses documents (anticipait-il leur publication?), il ne peut y avoir de doute qu'au cours des années quelque-uns de ceux-ci, du moins, ont été détruits ou irrémédiablement endommagés. D'autres, bien entendu, ont été perdus ou rejetés par ceux à qui ils étaient adressés. Nous pouvons, tout au plus, espérer combler les lacunes. Pour y parvenir, les documents d'importants personnages du temps du Riel feront l'objet de recherches afin de trouver des copies de ses lettres qui auraient pu être transcrites par d'autres personnes. Riel, hélas, a vécu avant l'invention des machines à photocopies. Lorsque les originaux ne sont pas accessibles, et s'il y a une très bonne raison de croire à l'authenticité de copies écrites à la main, elles seront incluses dans la publication avec mention de leur origine. De même façon, une recherche de journaux contemporains à Riel sera faite pour collectionner ses lettres aux éditeurs de divers journaux et qu'ils ont publiées.

Les essais inclus dans ce volume aideront à clarifier des aspects importants de Riel et de son temps. Riel était un personnage complexe et controversable et chaque nouveau livre ou nouvel article nous aide à saisir de façon plus complète les buts qu'il recherchait ainsi que les obstacles internes et externes semés le long de son parcours. Les membres du Projet Riel souhaitent sincèrement et même s'attendent à ce que la publication des écrits de Riel encourage les historiens de profession, comme les amateurs, à contribuer davantage à la compréhension de l'homme qui dirigea la cause des Métis en 1869 et en 1885.

1

Louis Riel As Charismatic Leader

Ken Hatt

Abstract

Weber's configurational model of charisma is posed as an alternative to the psychiatric and millenial perspectives which have been employed in previous studies of Riel. Three moments in the charismatic relation are suggested as applicable in interpreting his emergence in the 1885 insurrection. These are: the prophetic act; the establishment of charismatic authority; and charismatic domination.

The first is characterized by the emergence of a prophet who, through absolute commitment to a singular principle (value-rationality) systematizes his actions and calls others to do likewise. The possibility that these acts become a basis of duty through interaction with followers is seen in charismatic authority. This involves a process of interaction in which exceptional acts and their recognition lead to a social validation of the calling of the prophet. To the extent that such authority is organized (through the creation of a staff and a charismatic community) charismatic domination may be said to exist.

The implications of each of these moments for further research are explored. While no single principle of Riel's mission is explicit, one can be associated with the importance of the Métis nation and its achievement through the integration of political and religious activities. Further, the activity of Riel in late 1884 is interpreted as an effort to achieve the devotion of followers through revelations, deeds and exemplary behaviours. Finally, charismatic domination is briefly achieved through mobilization of troops and organizational activity (W.H. Jackson, the Exovedate). It is suggested that the final break with the clergy represents movement from a relation of authority to charismatic domination.

TO THE EXTENT that we address the person of Louis Riel, the Métis, we are confronted with the difficulty of finding a framework in which we can make his exceptional activity comprehensible. Toward that end, I take as my point of reference the Weberian concept of charisma and I will explore his activity as it culminated in the events of 1885.

The allotment of time prevents any more than a passing reference to two other approaches currently used in relation to Riel and the Métis. The first, based on psychiatric practice and insights, identifies Riel's behaviour as an aberration to be explained by subsuming it within a "syndrome". In what is probably the most explicit statement of this view, Markson (1965:249) judged Riel as psychotic "with predominantly manic and paranoid features". Flanagan (1977) has rightly criticized this approach, showing that the focus upon the insanity question avoids many of the critical questions regarding Riel.

A second view—the millenial perspective—has been suggested by Flanagan (1978). This involves identifying environmental factors associated with deprivation which, in turn, stimulates a reactive and intense transformation of a series of cultural beliefs. In the late nineteenth century, the Métis were a dislocated strata in the throes of adapting to the changing economic structure of the prairies. The decline of the buffalo and the fur trade as well as the increase in settlement had drastically affect their previous hunting and trading activities. In response to the abuse and incompetence of the Federal government, they joined in protest with the settlers. Hence, the protest grew from a wider agrarian base. The other Native strata—the Indian bands and the 'Half-breeds'—were more effectively subjected to the forces of neutralization. As Riel increasingly mobilized the Métis, the support of the white settlers diminished. I am suggesting that this is a movement which began, not as an indigenous cultural expression, but as part of an agrarian protest.

In addition, I would suggest that the expressions of Riel had little support even among the Métis. More specifically, it seems doubtful that his doctrines or beliefs were part of some indigenous cultural belief system. He did mobolize the Métis, but this was around one central principle: the defense and advancement of the Métis people. In Riel's expressions we are not talking, then, about a set of cultural beliefs with the scope or intensity of the Ghost dance.

In sum, we are dealing not so much with a millenial movement indigenous to the Métis as with the leading faction in a larger agrarian protest. And what we need to account for is how Riel mobilized this conspicuous sector. While the millenial model correctly addresses the conditions leading to the experience of deprivation, it requires the additional focus of Riel as the charismatic leader. This involves showing how Riel the prophet was creating and responding to the world on the level of meaning as an inherent part of this mobilization. Riel was a Métis intellectual. I suggest that an adequate comprehension of the man requires a view which enables us to see how his exceptional behavior (and it was exceptional) was progressively transformed in the process of mobilizing followers. Put simplistically, we need to avoid seeing him as either madman or victim.

The prophetic mission of Riel (the New Nation) requires explication not only in terms of the political and economic struggle on the prairies. It might be seen as a charismatic contrast to the bureaucratized conception embodied in Sir John A. Macdonald's National Policy. But rather than develop such an ambitious notion, I wish to interpret Riel with reference to what Weber called a "configurational model" of charisma.

Bendix (1971) and Rother (1975) have discussed three types of analytical procedure used by Weber. In research, Weber developed a number of exploratory (configurational) models like bureaucracy, feudalism, and charisma in his comparative study of socio-political processes. A more ambitious set of procedures (explanatory, or secular theories) were developed to account for the rise and decline of major historical events (Rother, 150). Finally, a third course of action (situational analysis) involved relating the explanatory theory to actual historical events, thus constituting a more exacting form of analysis.

In this paper I will briefly describe Weber's configurational model of charisma as it related to Riel in Saskatchewan. It is my contention that Weber's model of charisma may provide additional questions or insights on the man. I will proceed by outlining charisma in terms of three phases or moments in which it is constituted.

The first of these is the prophetic act; the second is the establishment of charismatic authority; and the third, charismatic domination. The contention is that through these notions we can follow the progressive transformation of Riel's action at the level of meaning.

The Prophetic Act:

The prototypical form of charismatic activity is found in Weber's (1968: 451) concept of prophecy. Prophecy consists of an individual claiming to bring new utterances (based on revelation) as a personal call to others. It involves a sense of mission, the proclamation of a doctrine which the prophet assumes as a personal calling. Examples of this are found among priests, magicians, lawgivers, ethical teachers and mystagogues. The act of prophecy may be expressed in teachings based on transcendant principles or through exemplary conduct.

The notion of the calling is not the only feature of the act of prophecy. It rests upon the fact that the prophet takes an integrated, meaningful attitude toward life. "To the prophet, both the life of man and the world, both social and cosmic events have a systematic and coherent meaning . . ." (Webber, 439 - 451). This meaning always contains the important religious conception of the prophet that the world as a cosmos should produce somehow a meaningful, ordered totality.

The content of this meaning may take varied forms. It may weld together into a unity, motives that are logically heterogeneous. The whole is dominated not by logical consistency, but by practical valuations. It is an effort to systematize all of life and organize it into commitment to a singular goal or principle.

In showing that orientations to the world may be seen as having a meaningful coherence, Weber (33-36) argued that two types of "rationality" were most significant: instrumental and value rationality. In the former, the actor orients himself by considering alternative means to achieve an end; the relative importance of various ends; and the relation of a goal to its secondary consequences. In other words, this is what we would typically consider "rational behaviour".

Value rationality refers to the situation in which the actor takes a particular value as supreme and orients his action systematically to this priority. Thus, the prophet achieves coherence in meaning through value-rationality: complete commitment to an absolute value which is systematically applied or sought in everyday life. While it thus becomes a guide for one's behaviour, it appears "irrational" from the point of view of instrumental rationality. And as Weber (450-451) noted

> "The conflict between empirical reality and this (value-rational) conception of the world as a meaningful totality which is based on the religious postulate, produces the strongest tensions in man's inner life as well as in his external relationship to the world".

The prophetic act as moment occurs when the prophet: a) assumes there is meaning to be found in the cosmos; b) finds it with reference to a principle which is of supreme worth; c) systematically applies it in day-to-day activity; and d) proclaims it as a call for others to follow.

Charismatic Authority:

While there are many prophetic acts, and actors, the problematic question is whether or not these claims are recognized or socially validated by others. This concerns the matter of charismatic authority.

The validity of charisma requires that the self-confidence of the leader and the devotion of the followers interact and reinforce one another (Schweitzer, 1974:153 passim.). Deeds and recognition are the two indispensable criteria for the validity of charisma. Calling and self-confidence initiate a claim, but recognition accepts the quality of the person and the exceptional deeds attest to the continued effectiveness of extraordinary power. When the devotion of the followers turns into a sense of duty, the prophetic act may be thought of as charismatic authority.

Charismatic Domination:

The perpetuation and organization of charismatic authority is what Weber (243-244) calls charismatic domination. This involves the establishment of a charismatic community primarily through the organization of a staff.

> The prophet has his disciples. There is only a call at the instance of the leader on the basis of charismatic qualification for a given task. The genuine prophet preaches, creates or demands new obligations—most typically by virtue of revelation, oracle, inspiration or of his own will.

The establishment of charismatic domination occurs as the leader, with the staff is capable of organizing on a regularized basis.

The three moments of charisma served only to summarize the vast amount of material found in Weber. The procedure I wish to follow is similar to that used by the proponents of the psychiatric and the millennial models. That is, "confirmation" is achieved by briefly outlining the elements of the model, then relating them to actual examples or empirical data. While Weber developed a much more powerful explanatory theory of charisma, I wish only to suggest that many of the prominent events associated with the Northwest Rebellion apply to the notion of charisma and Riel.

Perhaps the most problematic task is showing that Riel was acting with reference to a supreme goal or principle which was to be systematically related to in every-day life (value-rationality). I must admit much difficulty in this regard, but such a principle would revolve around the Métis as a people whose political integrity could not be constituted apart from the Church. It was a principle undoubtedly derived from Ultramontanism resting on the notion that religion and politics were inseparably wedded. The phases of his career which Flanagan (1974a, 1974b, 1975, 1976, 1977, 1978) has documented would be seen as involving the formulation and re-formulation of this principle in relation to the various tensions which this meaningful conception created.

When, in late 1884, he began to publicly issue his call to others, we see the transformation of his behaviour into the act of prophecy.

Reports of his increasing influence and authority are presented by various actors from a number of sources. Edgar Dewdney, Father Fourmond, Bishop Grandin, and Louis Schmidt all reported the emergence of interaction and mutual reinforcement bearing the marks of charismatic authority (Stanley: 1963: 274-291). Likewise, the competition between Riel and the clergy and the awareness of the latter of his growing influence (at their expense) has been widely documented. These two trends seem to constitute the bulk of his activity in the winter of 1884.

The resignation of W. H. Jackson as secretary of the Settlers Union to become Riel's personal secretary marks the potential onset of charismatic domination. Through mobilization of Dumont's military forces and the appointment of the Exovedate, the Provisional government becomes somewhat regularized. The Exovedate met daily, while it deliberated local matters and theological practicalities. Dumont desired an effective campaign of guerilla warfare, but Riel held him back, relying upon inspiration for his decisions. The charismatic domination was brief, but during this short period, Riel mobilized the force of the leading faction—and the remaining faction—of this agrarian protest.

As charismatic leader he mobilized the political/military forces and the religious intensities through leadership based on exemplary commitment to the notion of the Métis people. Riel, the Métis intellectual, forged the order around which the Métis people could be mobilized.

References:

Bendix, Reinhard, "Charismatic Leadership" in R. Bendix and G. Roth (ed.), *Scholarship and Partisanship;* Berkeley: University of California Press, 170-187, 1975.

Flanagan, Thomas, "Louis 'David' Riel: Prophet, Priest-King, Infallible Pontiff," *Journal of Canadian Studies, 9:15-25, 1974a.*

———*"Louis Riel's Religious Beliefs: A letter to Bishop* Taché," *Saskatchewan History,* 27:15-28, 1974b.

———"The Mission of Louis Riel," *Alberta History,* 23:1-12, 1975.

———*The Diaries of Louis Riel.* Edmonton: Hurtig Publishers, 1976.

———"Louis Riel: Insanity and Prophecy," in *The Settlement of the West.* Howard Palmer (ed.), Calgary: University of Calgary Press, 1977.

———"Catastrophe and the Millennium: A New View of Louis Riel," *Religion and Society in the Prairie West,* R. Allen (ed.), Regina: University of Saskatchewan, 35-51, 1978.

Roth, Guenther, "Socio-Historical Model and Developmental Theory," *American Sociological Review,* 40:148-157, 1975.

Schweitzer, Arthur, "Theory and Political Charisma," *Comparative Studies in Society and History,* 16:150-181, 1974.

Stanley, George F. G., *Louis Riel.* Toronto:McGraw-Hill Ryerson, Ltd., 1963.

Weber, Max, *Economy and Society.* Guenther Roth and Claus Wittich (ed.) New York: Bedminster Press, 1968.

2

Les Indiens dans la pensée messianique de Louis Riel

Gilles Martel

1. Le milieu et l'homme

La double population métisse

C'est vers la fin du XVIIIe siècle que le groupe métis de l'Ouest commença à prendre forme. Il dut son origine à l'établissement dans ces territoires des grandes compagnies qui s'adonnaient à la traite des fourrures avec les Indiens et dont les employés s'unirent à des Indiennes. Ce groupe métis se développa à partir de deux foyers distincts, géographiquement et linguistiquement. Le foyer septentrional—rives ouest et sud-ouest de la baie d'Hudson— où la Hudson's Bay Co. avait établi ses postes, donna naissance au groupe métis anglophone plutôt sédentaire. Le foyer méridional, où oeuvraient les compagnies rivales de la Hudson's Bay Co., donna naissance au groupe métis francophone de caractère beaucoup plus nomade. En effet, la Hudson's Bay Co. se contentait d'attendre les Indiens dans ses postes pour traiter avec eux, alors que les compagnies rivales envoyaient leurs hommes au milieu même des Indiens. Marcel Giraud a abondamment et minutieusement décrit l'origine et l'évolution de ces deux groupes métis (Giraud, 1945).

En 1812, Lord Selkirk fonda la colonie d'Assiniboia, partie sud de l'actuel Manitoba. Des Métis tant francophones qu'anglophones envahirent progressivement la colonie.

Selon Giraud (Giraud 1945:761), on aurait trois points de repère pour suivre

Année	Population blanche	Population métisse			Grand Total	% de la population Métisse
		Anglo	Franco	Total		
1838	1600			3400	5000	68%
1844	2000	1500	2500	4000	6000	66.7%
1857	1000	2000	4000	6000	7000	85.7%

l'évolution démographique de la population métisse dans la colonie.

En 1870, la population se répartissait ainsi selon les données du recensement officiel communiquées à Ottawa par le Lieutenant Gouverneur Archibald:

    5,720 Métis francophones
    4,080 Métis anglophones
    1,600 Blancs
     560 Indiens (établis et croyants)
    11,960

On peut donc parler d'une véritable colonie métisse: 81.9% de la population totale. Cependant même dans cette colonie existait une division socioculturelle du travail. Les Métis anglophones se concentraient dans des activités plus sédentaires, telles l'agriculture, le commerce et l'administration des postes de traite; les Métis francophones se spécialisaient dans des activités plus mobiles: grandes chasses au bison et transport de marchandises; plusieurs même hivernaient hors de la colonie.

Au cours de ces grandes chasses d'été et d'automne, ainsi que durant les hivernements hors de la colonie, les Métis francophones élisaient un rudimentaire "gouvernement provisoire" qui édictait et mettait en application ce qu'on appelait les "lois de la prairie". Les Métis francophones jouissaient donc d'une certaine structure politique spécifique parallèle à l'institution politique sommaire—gouverneur et conseillers—qui régissait l'ensemble de la colonie.

De plus, Métis francophones et Métis anglophones se concentraient dans des zones géographiques différentes à intérieur de la colonie et entretenaient assez peu de relations les uns avec les autres. Enfin l'un et l'autre groupes étaient encadrés jusqu'en 1870 par la seule structure paroissiale: catholique pour les Métis francophones, protestante pour les Métis anglophones (Martel, 1976:27-152). Il faut encore ajouter que d'autres Métis vivaient hors de la colonie, en contact étroit avec le monde indien et dispersés dans les vastes Territoires du Nord-Ouest.

Naissance de Louis Riel
Louis Riel naît le 22 ou le 23 octobre 1844 dans la colonie d'Assiniboia, plus

précisément dans la paroisse catholique et métisse canadienne-française de Saint-Boniface. Sa mère était canadienne-française et son père métis, petit-fils d'une Indienne montagnaise-chipewyan et d'un père canadien-français (Champagne, 1969). Son père s'était taillé une solide réputation de leader au sein des Métis francophones.

Séjour de Riel à Montréal

Dès l'âge de quatorze ans, le jeune Louis est envoyé par son évêque, Mgr Taché, au Collège de Montréal, pour y parfaire ses études classiques et se préparer au sacerdoce. Le 8 mars 1865, il est renvoyé du collège pour "infractions continuelles aux règles de la maison", vg. nombreuses absences de la pension et des classes (Lenoir, p.s.s., à Mgr Taché, cité dans Martel, 1976:174). En fait, il était tombé amoureux et se cherchait un emploi. Peu après, il connait une étrange expérience:

> "A l'âge de vingt ans, quand je venais de me jeter à côté du bon chemin, je fus un jour frappé soudainement et renversé sur le sol, presque sans vie. N'ayant pas encore fait de retraite pour ma décision, et étant inquiet au sujet de ma vocation, j'eus frayeur. Mais en tombant j'eus le temps de dire à Dieu: Seigneur, donnez-moi dix ans dans le monde et je le laisserai."(cité dans Martel, 1976:177).

Peut-être vers la même époque, il croit et affirme qu'il est Juif. Plusieurs années plus tard, il interprétera ses malheurs présents et passés comme une punition expiatoire pour cette défection. Il offre à Dieu, écrit-il à Mgr Taché, les sacrifices qui lui sont demandés "pour expier les quatre reniements dont, jeune encore, (il s'est) rendu coupable envers Dieu, envers la religion, envers (son) pays, envers (sa) famille", en se disant Juif. Cet épisode de la vie du jeune Riel reste assez obscur, quoique certains auteurs en ont fait presque un roman, (voir aussi Martel, 1976:199-207 et Campbell, Flanagan, Martel 1977:40-46).

Le soulèvement de 1869-70

Riel retourne dans son pays en 1868. En 1869-70, on le retrouve d'abord secrétaire puis président d'un mouvement de protestation contre le transfert de la colonie d'Assiniboia aux mains du gouvernement canadien. En effet, le gouvernement canadien, suite à de longues tractations avec le gouvernement britannique, avait obtenu que les Territoires du Nord-Ouest, jusque là sous la férule de la Hudson's Bay Co., passent sous sa juridiction. La date du transfert de juridiction est fixée au premier décembre 1960. En mai 1860, le gouvernement canadien vote un "acte concernant le gouvernement provisoire" de ces territoires. Puis il nomme le Lieutenant-Gouverneur (William McDougall) et certains membres de son conseil, tous extérieurs à la colonie. A la fin d'octobre 1869, McDougall et sa suite arrivent à Pembina. Ils y sont arrêtés par un groupe de Métis qui leur intime, au nom du *"comité na-tional des Métis* de la Rivière-Rouge (...) l'ordre de ne pas entrer sur le Ter-ritoire du Nord-Ouest sans une permission spéciale de ce comité". (voir Stanley, 1966:67-l07; Stanley, 1969:54-l56; Morton (ed.), 1956; Flanagan, 1978, sous presse.)

En fait, les Métis francophones avaient constitué ce comité et s'étaient donné comme objectif de protéger les terres communes et celles appartenant par entente "nationale" à telle partie de la population. En somme, ils enten-daient défendre comme leur *propriété collective* l'ensemble des terres qu'ils oc-cupaient, en tant que segment métis francophone. Plus tard, lorsqu'ils se seront emparés du Fort Garry, ils convaincront les Métis anglophones et les colons blancs de s'ériger avec eux en convention pour rédiger la liste des droits à négocier avec Ottawa. Ainsi ils exigeront d'Ottawa entre autres choses que la colonie d'Assiniboia entre dans la confédération canadienne à titre de province et non de simple "territoire" et ils demanderont pour les Métis une compensa-tion pour rachat de leur droit à la propriété du sol.

Suite à ces événements et surtout suite à l'exécution par le conseil de guerre métis de Thomas Scott, immigrant orangiste, Riel doit fuir son pays pour un certain temps. Jusqu'à la fin de 1873, même s'il vit dans une semi-retraite, il est élu député de Provencher au fédéral. Mais comme un mandat d'arrêt est émis contre lui, il fuit incognito vers l'Est.

La transformation radicale de l'Ouest

Le gouvernement canadien accorde le statut de province au Manitoba. Mais il laisse trainer en longueur le règlement de la question des terres métisses, v.g. extinction de leur droit à la propriété du sol. Or de 1870 à 1885, la physionomie du Manitoba se transforme radicalement. Un flot d'immigrants blancs en large majorité anglophones et protestants, se déverse sur le Manitoba, alors qu'une forte portion de la population métisse émigre plus à l'ouest et au sud, jusqu'aux Etats-Unis. Durant ces quinze ans la population du Manitoba décu-ple. Elle atteint 108,640 habitants en 1885-86. La population métisse qui représentait 82% de la population totale en 1870, ne représente plus que 7.3% de la population totale en 1885-86. La population métisse diminue même de l8.5% durant cette période. A ce changement démographique et par consé-quent culturel, d'autres transformations s'ajoutent. Le modèle d'occupation du sol se transforme rapidement: on s'éloigne des bordures des rivières, on abandonne le système d'encadrement paroissial pour le système municipal. Plusieurs agriculteurs s'orientent vers la monoculture du blé en vue de l'expor-tation. La ville de Winnipeg grossit à vue d'oeil et devient une véritable métropole: industries, magasins, hôtels s'y multiplient. Dans le domaine des transports, bateaux à vapeur et chemins de fer supplantent rapidement brigades de canots et de charrettes. Enfin, la disparition presque totale du bison durant ces années enlève aux Métis francophones leur principale source de subsistance et prive leur société des institutions qui la structuraient et la dynamisaient: gouvernement provisoire, lois de la prairie, grands rassemblements effervescents. On peut donc conclure qu'une crise d'évolution subite et profonde engendre dans la Société métisse une crise d'anomie non moins radicale (Martel, 1976:361-366).

Dès 1870, des Métis francophones commencent à s'installer sur la rivière Saskatchewan-Sud aux environs du Fort Carlton. Des Missionnaires oblats se joignent bientôt à eux et tentent de les convaincre de se convertir à l'agriculture, mais avec un succès très mitigé. En 1882, le père A. André souligne la pauvreté de plus en plus grande de la petite colonie métisse. En 1883-84, le père Fourmond, successeur du père André, parle de misère généralisée. La récolte est mauvaise, suite à la sécheresse, aux vers et aux gelées précoces. De plus, la crise économique mondiale fait sentir son effet jusque dans le Nord-Ouest: le frettage est à son minimum et la Hudson's Bay Co., profitant de la ruine de ses concurrents, engage les fréteurs métis à bas prix et les paie en marchandises de ses magasins et non en argent. L'hiver est extrêmement rigoureux et beaucoup de Métis fréteurs perdent un nombre considérable de leurs chevaux et sont souvent forcés d'abandonner leur charge le long du chemin. La mission reçoit de plus en plus de mendiants (Martel, 1976:366-376).

En fait, en 1883-84, c'est toute la population du Nord-Ouest canadien—Métis, Indiens et colons blancs—qui est victime de cette crise économique et qui tente par divers moyens d'exprimer ses griefs au gouvernement canadien pour obtenir son aide. Les colons anglophones—Blancs et Métis—, qui viennent de fonder la "Settlers' Union", vont contacter les Métis francophones. Après quelques rencontres, les deux parties s'entendent, au printemps 1884, pour envoyer une délégation à Louis Riel, qui réside alors au Montana, afin qu'il vienne les aider à rédiger leurs revendications auprès du gouvernement canadien (Martel, 1976:376-378).

Mais qu'est devenu, depuis 1870, l'homme politique, qui avait su forcer à l'époque, le gouvernement canadien à négocier l'entrée du Manitoba dans la confédération canadienne en tant que province?

II - Les Indiens dans la pensée messianique de Louis Riel

De 1870 à 1884, Riel avait connu de multiples déboires et tribulations qui l'avaient mené à la dépression nerveuse et...à l'illumination prophétique. Or ces révélation prophétiques de Riel sont de type messianique et millénariste. En d'autres mots, le message divin dont Riel se croit le dépositaire privilégié décrit les interventions divines dans l'histoire de l'humanité jusqu'à l'établissement définitif du Royaume de Dieu sur terre. Dans la tradition judéo-chrétienne, ces interventions divines se concentrent sur un peuple particulier que Dieu se choisit. Et c'est uniquement par un quelconque rattachement à ce peuple élu

que les autres peuples ont une chance de faire partie du Royaume. Le peuple
élu—et non seulement son chef—peut donc être considéré comme Messie,
i.e.comme sauveur, de l'humanité.

C'est en suivant l'évolution de cette pensée messianique de Riel que nous
pourrons mieux situer le rôle et la place que Riel entrevoyait pour le monde indien.

On peut diviser en quatre phases la genèse et l'évolution de cette pensée messianique de Riel. Première phase: l'élection divine et la révélation du plan de
l'action Dieu dans l'histoire de l'humanité (décembre 1875 - janvier 1878).
Deuxième phase: le rêve de reconquête de l'Ouest(1878 - juin 1884). Troisième
phase: la mise en marche du mouvement millénariste (juin 1884 - mai 1885).
Quatrième phase: la ré-interprétation de son message (mai - novembre 1885).

Première phase: l'élection divine et la révélation du plan de l'action de Dieu dans l'histoire de l'humanité (décembre 1875 - janvier 1878)

a) La grande synthèse messianique

En 1870-71, Riel doit fuir et se cacher pour échapper à la vindicte de ceux qui
veulent sa mort pour venger l'"exécution" par les Métis de l'orangiste on-
tarien Thomas Scott. Entre 1872 et 1875, il tente vainement d'entrer dans la
politique fédérale. Et même s'il est élu député à trois reprises, il ne peut jamais
occuper son siège au Parlement fédéral, toujours à cause de l'accusation du
meurtre de Scott qui pèse sur lui. En février 1875, le gouvernement canadien
vote à son sujet une amnistie conditionnelle. La condition? Il est privé de tous
ses droits politiques et banni pour cinq ans des territoires britanniques. Presque à bout de forces, il se réfugie aux Etats-Unis. Il s'adresse, sans succès,
d'abord aux féniens puis directement au Président Grant, cherchant de l'aide
pour reconquérir par la force l'Ouest canadien. Il est débouté là encore dans
ses efforts.

En décembre 1875, durant un séjour à Washington, débutent ses premières
expérences "mystiques". Il est convaincu que Dieu l'investit d'une mission de
salut universel, mais reliée au destin et à la mission de la nation métisse. Ses
parents et amis décident de le faire interner, d'abord à Saint-Jean-de-Dieu,
puis à Beauport. Il demeure en asile du 6 mars 1876 au 23 janvier 1878:"sa
communication avec Dieu, écrit-il, était continue et prise pour folie". Il se
considère comme "prêtre et roi de juridiction universelle", comme "pontife
infaillible" et comme "premier prophète du Nouveau-Monde", chargé d'annoncer les décrets de Dieu sur les nations, et, tel le Daniel des temps modernes,
de dévoiler les époques successives du Royaume de Dieu et la mission qu'y
jouera la nation métisse. Il se voit même comme le "messie de gloire
humaine".

Riel se situe lui-même explicitement dans la lignée des grands prophètes
d'Israël. A lui, comme à eux, affirme-t-il, est confiée la proclamation des
"décrets divins contre les empires du monde". A ses yeux, le monde est ac-

tuellement dominé par les grands empires infidèles et hérétiques, qui oppriment les nations catholiques. Or la cause des malheurs des nations catholiques, c'est le triomphe du "libéralisme". Si Dieu a permis que ce châtiment s'abbate sur elles c'est pour les punir et les corriger. Maintenant approche l'heure du démantèlement cataclysmique de ces empires. Le Vieux-Monde est sur le point de s'embraser. Et la papauté doit quitter Rome.

Dieu, pourtant, a choisi une nouvelle Terre Promise, l'Amérique, et un nouveau Peuple Elu, le peuple canadien-français et son rejeton, le peuple métis canadien-français. La mission du peuple métis succédera à celle de la nation canadienne-française qui, elle-même, continue "les grands travaux de la France de ce côté-ci de la mer".

Dans la synthèse messianique de Riel, les Métis canadiens-français sont appelés à constituer le peuple sacerdotal dans les derniers temps de la troisème période du "Royaume de Dieu". La première période fut celle de l'Eglise et du sacerdoce juif, la seconde, celle de l'Eglise et du sacerdoce catholique romain, la troisième sera celle, d'abord de l'Eglise et du sacerdoce canadien-français de Montréal, puis celle de l'Eglise et du sacerdoce métis canadien-français de Saint-Vital, paroisse manitobaine de résidence de la famille Riel.

Selon sa supputation du temps, la troisième et dernière période du Royaume de Dieu, i.e. celle du Royaume de Dieu en Amérique, est appelée à durer 2333 ans (1876-4209), soit 457 ans pour la sous-époque de l'Eglise Canadienne-française de Montréal (1876-2333) et 1876 ans pour la sous-époque de l'Eglise métisse canadienne-française de Saint-Vital (2333-4209).

Durant cette troisième période, celle du Royaume de Dieu en Amérique, sera rétablie la loi mosaïque et en particulier la polygamie qui permettra au peuple métis de se multiplier rapidement. D'ailleurs, ce peuple métis se recrutera "du mélange de tous les sangs entr'eux" et constituera une nouvelle nation qui devra se couler "dans le moule canadien-français" pour s'assimiler les moeurs, coutumes et traditions françaises et catholiques. Pourtant chacune de ces ethnies, après ce moulage, conservera un certain "souvenir de son origine, origine, en s'appelant métisse". Ce sera enfin l'unité dans la diversité! (Martel, 1976:253-310.)

b) *Le mythe de l'origine hébraïque des Indiens*

On peut maintenant situer et décrire la place que tenait le monde indien dans cette première synthèse messianique de Riel. Le sang indien, dont une partie coule dans les veines des Métis de l'Ouest canadien, est du plus pur sang d'Abraham, affirme Riel.

Le 20 avril 1876, alors qu'il est à l'asile de La-Longue-Pointe, Riel écrit à Mgr Bourget que le Saint-Esprit lui "a révélé que les Sauvages de l'Amérique du Nord sont Juifs et du plus pur sang d'Abraham". Plus tard, il affirmera qu'il eut cette révélation au mois de février précédent, alors qu'il résidait encore chez son oncle, John Lee.

Il raconte en effet à Mgr Bourget qu'à l'époque de la naissance de Moïse un bateau égyptien, ayant à son bord vingt-sept Egyptiens et dix-sept Hébreux, des tribus de Zabulon et de Ruben, aborda en Amérique, après une errance de 18 mois sur les mers. Les Hébreux voulaient fuir l'Egypte pour se rendre en Asie, dans la Terre promise à la postérité d'Abraham. Après une violente tempête, ils tentèrent vainement de reprendre leur route vers l'est, mais acceptèrent, sur la parole d'une petite fille, l'dée que la Terre Promise se trouvait à l'ouest et mirent résolument le cap sur le soleil couchant. Leur bateau aborda au Mexique le 13 avril après l'année de la naissance de Moïse. Du 13 avril au 25 janvier suivant, Hébreux et Egyptiens restèrent ensemble. Puis, les Egyptiens demandèrent aux Hébreux de leur donner comme épouses leurs filles les plus âgées et poussèrent les Hébreux vers le nord. Ainsi les Indiens du nord de l'Amérique sont du plus pur sang d'Abraham, alors que dans les veines des Indiens du Mexique, de l'Amérique centrale et de l'Amérique du Sud coule du sang égyptien mêlé au sang d'Abraham.

Notons que le thème de la migration d'un ''reste d'Israël'' est un thème récurrent dans l'histoire des doctrines messianiques et millénaristes du monde judéo-chrétien.

Fondamentalement, cette croyance repose sur une espérance messianique israélite selon laquelle le Messie rassemblera dans la Terre Sainte les *douze* tribus d'Israël. En effet, on se rapelle que, suite à la défaite d'Israël, les rois d'Assyrie déportèrent dans leur pays la majorité des fils d'Israël. Or, seul un reste de deux tribus d'Israël (Juda et Lévi ou Benjamin) revint s'installer en Palestine avec Esdras et Néhémie. Pourtant, selon une interprétation littérale des Prophètes, c'est tout Israël, i.e. les douze tribus, qui doit revenir en Terre Sainte pour jouir de l'ère messianique. Donc, selon cette croyance, il était impossible que les dix autres tribus d'Israël aient été anéanties: elles devaient se trouver quelque part, sous un autre nom, attendant que le Messie les rassemble. S'appuyant sur cette croyance, beaucoup d'auteurs cherchèrent à localiser les descendants de ces dix tribus d'Israël, en Arabie, aux Indes, en Abyssinie, en Europe, au Japon, etc., et enfin en Amérique (The Jewish Encyclopedia, au mot ''Tribes, lost ten'').

La plus connue de ces théories de l'origine israélite des Indiens d'Amérique est sans doute celle de Joseph Smith dans le *Livre de Mormon*.

Pourtant au XIXe siècle, l'idée que les Indiens de l'Amérique fussent de descendance juive était fort répandue au point que Thomas F.O'Dea, dans son étude sur les Mormons, pouvait écrire: ''To the popular notions of Hebraic genesis, the Book of Mormon added nothing new'' (O.Dea, 1968:25). On pourrait être tenté de croire que Riel s'est inspiré du *Livre de Mormon* pour rédiger son texte sur l'origine juive des Indiens d'Amérique, mais si on compare le récit de Riel au *Livre de Mormon,* on trouve trop de différences substantielles pour que le dernier ait inspiré le premier.

Deuxième phase: le rêve de reconquête de l'Ouest (1878 - juin 1884)
Riel sort de l'asile de Beauport le 23 janvier 1878. Il s'installe chez son ami le curé Fabien Barnabé de Keeseville. Il tombe amoureux de la soeur du curé, Evelina.

Pendant les mois qui suivent, il affirme à plusieurs de ses parents et amis qu'il a renoncé à toute action politique pour se consacrer à l'agriculture. Pourtant, dès l'automne suivant, il se rend à New York dans l'intention de se chercher un emploi, mais aussi pour se procurer de l'argent afin de réaliser son "but patriotique", "son oeuvre du Nord-Ouest", affirme son ami le curé Barnabé. A New York, il aurait contacté un groupe de Féniens, mais n'aurait rien obtenu d'eux (Flanagan, sous presse, chap. 5:3-5).

De plus, ses illuminations intérieures n'ont pas cessé complètement. Mais ses années d'asile lui ont appris à être plus discret à leur sujet.

a) L'espoir de soulever les Indiens
En décembre 1878, on retrouve Riel au Minnesota, hanté par l'idée d'une action violente contre les Anglais du Manitoba. Désespéré de ne pouvoir obtenir l'aide des Américains, il ne compte plus que sur les Indiens. Dans un poème, titulé "En voyant Minnesota" écrit le 26 décembre 1878, il dit ses espoirs de vengeance. Il lui apparait que le Manitoba a été mis "sous le joug du peuple abâtardi", i.e. les Anglais venus de l'Ontario, et que ces nouveaux venus cherchent à modeler à leur façon la destinée de la nouvelle province. Il crie à son peuple qu'il est prêt à venir le venger en appelant à son secours les "nations sauvages" de la région du Missouri. C'est son désir le plus cher. Pourtant, il hésite encore car Dieu ne lui a pas donné de signe manifeste que c'est là sa volonté, conclut-il.

Les années 1878, 1879 et 1880 sont parmi les plus catastrophiques dans l'histoire des Indiens du Nord-Ouest: le bison a presque totalement disparu des prairies et même le petit gibier se fait rare. Hantés par le spectre de la famine et du désespoir, des milliers d'Indiens traversent la frontière à la poursuite des derniers troupeaux de bisons qui paissent encore dans la région du Missouri et du Judith Basin.

Selon le Surintendant Walsh stationné au poste de la Police Montée à la Montagne-de-Bois, Riel aurait signé, à l'automne 1879, une sorte de traité avec les Indiens Assiniboines et leur chef Red Stone de la Montagne-de-Bois. Ce document stipulait que le pays appartenait aux Indiens et à leurs frères les Métis, que Riel était leur vrai chef et que, si les Indiens acceptaient de s'unir sous son autorité, il pourrait reconquérir leurs terres grâce à l'appui politique de ses amis de l'est du Canada et des Etats-Unis (Flanagan, sous presse, ch. 5:13-14).

Au cours de l'hiver 1879-1880, selon un autre témoignage, Riel aurait profité de la situation critique des Indiens pour tenter de les soulever contre le

Canada. Il aurait même tenté de les embrigader dans un vaste projet d'invasion et de prise de possession des Territoires du Nord-Ouest canadien. Ces Territoires, aurait-il proclamé, étant la propriété naturelle des Indiens et des Métis, ils devaient être mis à part pour leur usage exclusif et gouvernés par eux seuls, selon leurs lois. Indiens et Métis auraient uni leurs forces pour s'emparer du Fort de la Montagne-de-Bois, du Fort Walsh, du Fort Macleod et enfin de Battleford. Les Indiens habitant les territoires américains auraient également été invités à participer à ce vaste soulèvement. Une fois Battleford aux mains des Métis et des Indiens, Riel aurait proclamé le Gouvernement provisoire. Le rassemblement général des troupes avait été fixé au mois de mai 1880, à Tiger Hills, sur la Milk River. Et les troupes d'invasion devaient se mettre en marche dès le début de juin.

Riel aurait dévoilé les détails de ce projet à Jean L'Heureux, espérant que ce dernier l'aiderait à convaincre Crowfoot, le chef des Indiens Pieds-Noirs. Or, l'Heureux agissait alors comme une sorte d'agent secret du gouvernmement canadien, l'Heureaux, après avoir poussé les Pieds-Noirs à s'éloigner des Métis, avertit les autorités civiles et militaires du Montana. Avant la réunion de mai, les autorités, après avoir imposé des restrictions sur le commerce des munitions, auraient expédié un corps de troupe vers Tiger Hills. Riel et ses Métis (200 familles) durent fuir vers Judith Basin. Là, il aurait attendu la fin de la campagne du général Nelson Miles contre les Sioux pour soulever à nouveau les Indiens. Malheureusement, nous ne possédons aucun document de Riel lui-même qui confirmerait ou infirmerait ce témoignage de L'Heureux (Martel, 1976:322-323).

Enfin, selon le témoignage de Joseph Poitras, au cours de l'hiver 1880-81, Riel rencontra plusieurs Métis et Indiens des Territoires du Nord-Ouest en hivernant à la Milk River. Riel vint de Yellowstone pratiquer la traite au milieu d'eux. "Plusieurs assemblées se tinrent alors, tous manifestant leur mécontentement". Les Métis se plaignaient au sujet de leurs terres et les Indiens au sujet de leurs traités avec le gouvernement canadien. Riel affirmait que le gouvernement canadien avait obtenu les terres des Indiens pour une bagatelle et qu'il ne tenait pas les promesses qu'il avait faites tant aux Indiens qu'aux Métis. "Il leur recommandait aussi de se tenir unis ensemble, et unis au clergé, prêts à faire valoir leurs droits". De plus, Riel ayant constaté que les bisons disparaissaient rapidement, insistait auprès d'eux pour qu'ils aillent prendre des terres et s'y établissent. Beaucoup de Métis suivirent son conseil et allèrent prendre des terres sur les bords de la Saskatchewan (Martel, 1976:323-324).

D'autre part, il est certain que Riel personnellement ou par des intermédiares, est entré en contact avec Sitting Bull et ses Indiens Sioux. Riel affirme qu'il s'efforçait de pacifier les Sioux. Mais par ailleurs, il est certain qu'il encouragea Sitting Bull et sa "bande" à s'installer au Canada. Riel voulait-il utiliser à son avantage l'agressivité des Indiens Sioux en la dirigeant contre le

Canada? C'est possible et même probable.

b) Le projet d'une république théocratique métisse assimilant pacifiquement les Indiens
Suite à l'échec de sa tentative de soulever les Indiens, il semble que Riel se soit consacré exclusivement à tâcher de défendre et d'améliorer le sort des Métis. Il veut les protéger à la fois contre les voleurs de chevaux et les trafiquants d'alcool; il cherche aussi à leur obtenir des "réserves" afin de les sédentariser et de les convertir à l'agriculture. Pour obtenir quelque appui des Blancs, il se lance dans la mêlée politique. Mal lui en prend car il est accusé d'avoir incité à voter des Métis qui n'ont pas le droit de vote. Cette affaire traîne jusqu'au 16 avril 1884, alors que le procès est renvoyé faute de preuve (Martel, 1976:325-329).

En avril 1882, alors qu'il réside près de la mission jésuite de St. Peter, Montana, Riel décrit ainsi la situation des Métis des environs.

> "Les missionnaires de la mission St.-Pierre, près de Fort Shaw, ont établi il y a cinq ans une colonie métisse autour de leur établissement. Et ils font tout en leur pouvoir pour encourager ces nouveaux colons à l'agriculture pour qu'ils atteignent à une vie plus prospère (...)
> Il y a à la mission Saint-Pierre, près de Fort Shaw environ 25 familles métisses qui s'efforcent de s'établir comme fermiers. Il y a cinquante familles métisses établies dans "Judith Basin" et ses environs. Il y en avait 70 établies dans le voisinage de "Wilder's Landing" l'hiver dernier, et 80 autres à l'embouchure de la "Musselshell" et plus bas vers "Fort Peck". Et combien d'autres familles qui vivent isolées et dispersées dans tout le Territoire?" (Helena Weekly Herald, 26 avril 1883.)

Le 18 décembre 1883, il commence à enseigner à l'école de la mission St. Peter.

C'est aussi vers cette date qu'il aurait confié au major Alex C. Botkin son projet de lancer "un mouvement pour l'indépendance des Métis et l'établissement d'une république dans les provinces (sic) d'Assiniboia et de la Saskatchewan". Riel lui aurait même dit avoir déjà mis par écrit une constitution et un plan détaillé pour l'exécution de ce projet.

Dans son esprit, les Métis constituaient véritablement un peuple et il projetait de rassembler tous les Métis des Etats-Unis et des territoires britanniques de l'Amérique du Nord pour bâtir avec eux une nation dont le gouvernement serait à la fois de type républicain et théocratique. Le catholicisme y serait reconnu constitutionnellement comme la seule vraie foi, mais après répudiation de l'autorité de Rome (Botkin, 1900).

D'autres documents nous permettent de confirmer et de compléter ce témoignage de Botkin. Voyons d'abord la représentation que Riel se fait des Métis comme peuple. Au cours de l'été 1883, il compose deux textes sur ce thème: une ode, "Le peuple métis-canadien-français" et une lettre adressée à Pierre Lavallée. Dans l'un et l'autre textes, il affirme en somme que le peuple métis, résultat de l'amalgame des sangs français, canadiens-français et indiens, participe aux qualités de ces trois groupes pour constituer un peuple original, destiné à devenir le "porte-enseigne"

> "Du droit naturel qu'on dédaigne
> Et qu'on met partout en oubli." (L'Echo du Manitoba, 23 juin 1898.)

C'est probablement à cette époque que Riel commence à rêver d'un métissage global de tout l'Ouest canadien. Probablement influencé par le programme de Mgr Ireland, il entrevoit une immigration italienne, irlandaise, bavaroise et polonaise dans le Nord-Ouest canadien. Les immigrants de chacun de ces peuples occuperaient une portion spécifique du territoire et s'amalgameraient avec les tribus indiennes de ces régions. "Ainsi toute la race sauvage de l'Amérique du Nord ferait place à une race nouvelle: la race métisse qui varierait selon les pays". Race métisse canadienne-française au Manitoba, race métisse irlandaise en Nouvelle-Irlande, race métisse italienne en Nouvelle-Italie, race métisse bavaroise en Nouvelle-Bavière, race métisse polonaise en Nouvelle-Pologne.

Riel insiste sur l'importance de la religion catholique pour le peuple métis

> "Le Métis comprend que *l'Eglise*
> *Est Reine à la tête de tout*
> Que du Ciel étant la commise
> Ses oeuvres seuls restent debout."

A ces textes, on peut ajouter ce couplet d'une autre chanson à la gloire des Métis.

> "Chez les Métis, l'Etat, l'Eglise
> De tout temps n'ont jamais fait qu'un
> Tous deux avaient pour entreprise
> De sauver les droits de chacun
> Quand l'Eglise était offensée
> L'etat se trouvait affligé
> Et la nation menacée
> Avait l'appui de son clergé."

Il est sûr qu'à cette époque, Riel est encore convaincu de la répudiation de Rome. Il écrit dans un brouillon de lettre à Mgr Bourget que "le Saint-Esprit a laissé Rome, comme Rome l'avait laissé la première". Et il poursuit en affirmant que la grâce pontificale n'est plus en Léon XIII, mais dans la personne de Mgr Bourget. Cependant, pour se séparer de Rome, il faut attendre le mot

d'ordre de Jésus-Christ lui-même.
    On peut situer à cette époque la diatribe suivante:

> "Et vous! Grande ville de Rome
> (...)
> Par leurs finesses vos Pontifes
> Ne sont plus que des vieux pachas
> Ils ont au bout des doigts des griffes
> Malignes comme en ont les chats
> "Méchante je vous incrimine
> Devant le tribunal de Dieu
> Plaise au Christ qu'on vous extermine
> Au milieu du soufre et du feu.''

Riel entrevoit de doter ce nouveau peuple métis d'une forme de gouvernement républicain copiée sur le gouvernement des Etats-Unis. "Toutes ces nations métisses canadienne-française, italienne, irlandaise, bavaroise et
polonaise apprendraient de Washington l'art de gouverner, comme les nations
européennes ont jadis appris de l'empire romain l'obéissance et le commandement''.
    Pour assurer l'harmonie dans cette diversité, il propose que les "chefs
d'armée'', les chefs des "prêtres et des ministres'' et les chefs politiques (?) de
toutes ces nations se réunissent en trois conseils distincts, et, qu'une fois tous
les trente ans, ces trois conseils se réunissent en une vaste convention dans le
but de faire "un grand acte d'amitié chrétienne et un grand pas vers la con-
corde universelle'' (Martel, 1976:331-336).
    En même temps qu'il élabore ce vaste projet utopique, il se replie dans un ef-
fort ascétique et se concentre sur une réflexion philosophico-théologique. Toujours convaincu d'avoir une mission politoco-religieuse à remplir face à la
répudiation divine de Rome (répudiation prononcée, mais non encore effective), à la réforme du catholicisme et au salut du monde à travers la "nation''
métisse, il tâche de s'y préparer par l'ascèse, couche par écrit ses réflexions en
vue d'une publication éventuelle et espère ardemment le signe divin annonçant
l'abandon effectif de Rome et confirmant ainsi ses révélations. Mais comme le
temps passe, des doutes s'insinuent dans son esprit: "Qui suis-je pour essayer
à mener les événements? Un néant, c'est moi!'' (Martel, 1976:336-348).

**Troisième phase: la mise en march du mouvement millénariste
(juin 1884-mai 1885)**
a) Enfin! un premier signe providentiel
Le 4 juin 1884, Riel reçoit une délégation des Métis du Nord-Ouest, venant lui
demander de leur prêter secours dans leurs revendications auprès d'Ottawa.
Riel interprète l'arrivée de cette délégation comme un signe providentiel. Selon
Michel Dumas, un des délégués, Riel leur aurait déclaré solennellement:

"Comme si Dieu me trouvait assez préparé voici que vous venez me chercher.—Rien n'arrive sans son ordre et sa permission. Et la visite que vous me faites me vient de Lui. Je remercie Dieu de me permettre de recommencer comme de plus bel." (Martel, 1976:354)

De plus, vers la même date, il reçoit une lettre d'un de ses cousins lui expliquant la situation en Saskatchewan et lui annonçant l'arrivée de la délégation. La lettre précise même: "J'ai la certitude que (en acceptant de venir nous aider) tu feras un effort suprême avec la protection du Dieu de toutes les nations et de toutes gloires. (...) L'histoire te mettra au rang des plus grands héros de cette époque" (Martel, 1976:353).

Tout cela ne pouvait que le confirmer dans ses convictions et le rassurer dans ses espérances.

b) Le sang indien comme titre à la propriété du sol

Les délégués exposent à Riel le but de leur mission, en lui présentant leurs lettres de créances et la liste des griefs et revendications au sujet desquels ils viennent le consulter. Ils lui présentent aussi un document qui l'invite à venir au Nord-Ouest.

La liste des griefs et revendications apportée par la délégation étant perdue, on peut en reconstituer la substance grâce à deux autres documents légèrement antérieurs. Notons que dans ces deux documents les gens du Nord-Ouest ne réclament aucun droit spécifiquement métis, mais seulement des droits individuels de squatters, pour les Métis comme pour les colons blancs.

C'est Riel qui introduira dans leurs revendications l'affirmation que les Métis ont un droit spécifique et collectif de propriété sur tous les "territoires du Nord-Ouest" au titre de leur sang indien et ceci, en sus de leurs droits individuels de squatters.

Pour Riel, cela signifie que les Métis, en tant que peuple, sont copropriétaires du sol avec le peuple indien, et cela précisément au titre de leur sang indien. Cela signifie encore, selon lui, qu'en 1870, les Métis n'ont cédé leur droit de propriété qu'à l'intérieur des limites du Manitoba d'alors et qu'en conséquence, de nouvelles négociations sont nécessaires pour étendre leur droit de propriété sur le reste des Territoires du Nord-Ouest.

S'appuyant sur ce principe, Riel réclamera—dans un mémorandum à Mgr Grandin pour qu'il l'achemine à Ottawa—que "deux millions d'acres soient mis à part par le gouvernement pour le bénéfice des Métis, protestants et catholiques. Que le gouvernement vende ces terres; qu'il en dépose l'argent à la banque, et que l'intérêt de cet argent serve au soutien des écoles, à la construction d'orphelinats et d'hôpitaux, à l'entretien des maisons de ce genre déjà construites; et pour procurer aux Métis pauvres des charrues et tous les printemps de quoi ensemencer la terre". Et à partir de ce moment Riel s'efforce d'évaluer en argent ces terres métisses et indiennnes ainsi que le taux d'intérêt que ce placement devrait rapporter. (Martel 1976:389-406)

c) L'idéologie messianique ésotérique et la fondation de'Exovidat
Depuis son arrivée en Saskatchewan, Riel reste très discret sur sa doctrine messianique. Pourtant, il s'efforce de convertir un petit groupe d'élus à ses idées que nous connaissons déjà.

Il formule même une théorie de la double papauté. D'après ses révélations, l'Esprit-Saint a investi Mgr Bourget de la papauté depuis le 8 décembre 1875. Mais jusqu'à ce que Dieu fournisse un signe indéniable, c'est la double papauté (Martel, 1976:4ll).

D'autre part, il ne perd pas de vue l'autre élément de sa doctrine messianique, soit la fondation de ce qu'on pourrait appeler les Etats-Unis métis du Nord-Ouest. Pour s'assurer une large immigration des ethnies européenes installées aux Etat-Unis qui viendront composer cette nouvelle nation métisse—après l'avoir aidée à s'emparer du Nord-Ouest—Riel a besoin d'un puissant organe de publicité. Il songe à la fondation d'un journal aux Etats-Unis. Mais pour fonder un journal il lui faut de l'argent; il demande alors une indemnité monétaire au gouvernement canadien par l'intermédiaire du père André et d'un membre du Conseil du Nord-Ouest, indemnité destinée à compenser les dommages que le gouvernement canadien lui avait fait subir depuis 1870. Ottawa ne daigne même pas répondre à cette demande (Martel, 1976:426-430).

Riel commence à trouver que les choses traînent en longeur et déclare qu'il est temps de montrer les dents. Le premier mars 1885, il demande aux Métis de venir à une assemblée "en armes". Dans les jours qui suivent, il fait signer à certains Métis un engagement à prendre les armes pour "la gloire de Dieu, l'honneur de la religion et le salut des âmes". Riel veut même proclamer un gouvernement provisoire pour revenir en quelque sorte à la situation de 1870. A son avis, le gouvernement canadien n'ayant pas respecté ses engagements de 1870, les Métis sont dans leur droit en rétablissant leur gouvernement provisoire pour reprendre leurs négociations avec Ottawa.

Pendant ce temps, à Prince-Albert, on s'inquiète de cette agitation métisse. Une troupe d'une centaine d'hommes est levée et se met en marche le 18 mars.

Les Métis forment un conseil, raflent les armes et munitions qu'ils peuvent trouver, prennent des prisonniers en otages. Ils s'installent dans l'église Saint-Antoine de Batoche. Riel proclame: "Rome est tombée. L'Eglise romaine a besoin de réforme et je suis appelé à la réformer. L'Esprit m'a dit ce matin: Va délivrer ton peuple" (Martel, 1976:442-444). Les Métis décident de s'emparer du Fort Carlton et demandent sa reddition sans condition.

Désormais, ce conseil métis s'appellera *Exovidat* (de *"ex"* et *"ovile"*, "tiré du troupeau", selon Riel). Ce conseil a toute autorité politique, militaire et même religieuse. Riel n'en fait pas partie directement: il en est le prophète officiel, en contact direct avec Dieu, et il communique ses "révélations" au conseil *(Exovidat)* qui prend ses décisions à vote majoritaire.

Riel et l'*Exovidat* s'efforcent de convaincre les anglophones de se joindre à eux. Ils font aussi appel aux Indiens.

Le 26 mars, au Lac-au Canard, les Métis rencontrent la colonne de policiers et de volontaires de Prince-Albert. Suite à un faux mouvement, la fusillade s'engage. La colonne des policiers et volontaires doit battre en retraite (Martel, 1976:453-454). Il n'y aura pas d'autre engagement avant le 24 avril.

Durant ce temps l'*Exovidat* est surtout occupé à des discussions religieuses. (Martel, 1976: 456-472; Flanagan. 1974 c: 35-52.)

Les Métis comptent environ 250 à 300 hommes peu et mal armés. A la fin de mars, le gouvernement canadien lève une armée d'environ 8,000 hommes pour mâter les Métis, et aussi les Indiens qui commencent à se soulever. Première bataille, le 24 avril à Fish Creek: les Métis y perdent cinq hommes. Du 9 au 12 mai, l'armée attaque les Métis retranchés à Batoche. A bout de munitions, les Métis sont vaincus et perdent une douzaine d'hommes. Le 15 mai, Riel se rend au général Middleton de l'armée canadienne (Martel, 1976: 482—488).

d) Place et rôle des Indiens dans le soulèvement

Riel et l'*Exovidat* sont très conscients de la petitesse et de la faiblesse de leurs effectifs. C'est pourquoi ils s'efforcent de convaincre, tant les Métis anglophones que leurs frères métis éloignés, de se joindre à eux. Mais Riel rêve surtout d'un large renfort indien. Dans les premières semaines d'avril, il note dans son journal cette prière: "Daignez les (Indiens) envoyer tous à mon secours", de l'est, de l'ouest, du nord et du sud, qu'ils "nous arrivent très bientôt munis de bonnes armes et d'une grande quantité de munitions", espoir qui ne se réalisera pas.

Les Métis anglophones, tout en se déclarant sympathiques à la cause refusent de prendre les armes. Les Métis francophones des régions plus éloignées se tiennent cois. Quant aux Indiens, selon le témoignage du Métis Michel Dumas, il en serait venu 68 dans le camp métis, soit 43 de la réserve Beardy et 15 de la réserve One Arrow (Martel, 1976: 483). Les autres Indiens, qui déterrent la hache de guerre, ne se joignent pas au camp métis mais mènent leurs opérations de leur côté (Stanley, 1966: 332—349).

Quantrième phase: la ré-interprétation de son message (mai-novembre 1885)
a) Nouvel auditoire, nouvel espoir

Le 15 mai 1885, Riel se rend au général Middleton; le 23 mai, il entre à la prison de Regina. Son procès se déroule du 20 juillet au 1er août alors qu'il est condamné à être pendu le 18 septembre 1885. L'exécution de la sentence est remise à trois reprises. Le 16 novembre 1885, il monte à l'échafaud.

Durant cette période, Riel s'efforce de saisir toutes les occasions qui se présentent pour lancer à tous azimuts tant ses revendications socio-politiques pour son peuple, que son utopie du peuplement du Nord-Ouest et son message de réforme du christianisme. Il sait qu'il a enfin capté l'attention d'un auditoire immense et même international et il ne peut laisser passer une telle occasion.

Riel espère même que son proceès se déroulera en français au Québec, devant la Cour Suprême, et qu'il donnera lieu à un exposé complet de la politique du gouvernement canadien vis-à-vis le Nord-Ouest, les Métis et lui-même. Or son procès se déroulera à Regina, en anglais, devant un simple juge stipendié et six jurés. On n'y discutera que son rôle dans les trois batailles du Lac-au-Canard, de la Couleé des Tourond et de Batoche. A sa grande surprise, et même à son désespoir, ses avocats plaideront la folie. Mais Riel profitera de l'occasion qui lui sera offerte à la fin de son procès, pour exposer encore une fois ses vues et ses revendications.

Du moment de sa reddition jusqu'à sa pendaison, il revise, réajuste et même parfois ré-interprète son message tant socio-politique que religieux, en fonction, bien souvent, de l'auditoire auquel il s'adresse.

b) Le droit des Métis au septième (1/7) des terres du Nord-Ouest
Selon Riel, les Métis conservent leur droit à la propriété du sol des Territoires du Nord-Ouest même dupuis l'acquisition des Territoires par le Canada. Ce principe, il l'expose dans une interview au *New York Herald,* le 26 mai 1885. Ce droit, affirme-t-il, est le même aujourd'hui qu'avant le transfert des Territoires du Nord-Ouest au gouvernement canadien. Riel reconnait que la Compagnie de la Baie d'Hudson a vendu ses intérêts dans le pays, mais les Métis n'appartiennent pas à la Compagnie, et en conséquence, pourrait-on poursuivre, la Compagne n'a pu aliéner leurs droits. Il est encore vrai, dit-il, que les Indiens, ceux du moins qui ont fait des traités avec le gouvernement canadien, ont vendu leurs intérêts dans le pays. Mais les Métis, en dehors du Manitoba, n'ont pas vendu ni transféré leurs droits: ils n'ont pas non plus abandonné leur forme de gouvernement provisoire, ni reconnu le gouvernement canadien dans ces territoires. Ils sont prêts, cependant, à conclure un traité équitable avec le gouvernement canadien sur la base de celui du Manitoba et à entrer dans la Confédération.

Dans son discours, à la fin de son procès, Riel explicite sur quel principe de droit naturel et divin repose, selon lui, la revendication des Métis à la propriété du sol:

> En Angleterre, en France, les Anglais, les Français possèdent le sol. Les premiers qui furent en Angleterre devinrent les propriétaires du sol, et ils l'ont transmis de génération en génération. Par le sol, il sont devenus une nation. Qui fait les nations? Le même qui les a créées, Dieu. Dieu est le maître de l'univers, notre planète est sa terre, et les nations et les tribus sont les membres de sa famille, et, comme un bon père, il donne une portion de ces terres à cette nation, à cette tribu, à chacun de cette nation, de cette tribu, c'est son héritage, c'est sa part d'héritage.''

Mais qu'arrive-t-il lorsqu'une nation, qui a eu sa part d'héritage, "s'est multipliée de telle sorte qu'elle a encombré son pays, (et) qu'il ne lui reste plus d'espace chez elle"?

> il ne lui est pas permis de prendre la part de la petite tribu à côté d'elle. Quand elle vient, elle devrait dire: ma petite soeur, tribu des Cris, vous avez un vaste territoire qui vous a été donné, c'est votre propriété, tout comme il en a été donné (un) en Angleterre, en France. Vous ne pouvez exister sans cette terre.

Riel interrompt brusquement son raisonnement, mais on peut facilement y suppléer: ces nouveaux venus doivent négocier pacifiquement une entente équitable avec les légitimes possesseurs du sol.

Riel modifiera à plusieurs reprises son évaluation en argent des terres "indiennes" et "métisses", mais ce dont Riel a besoin, c'est une base de calcul fixe, qui lui permette d'évaluer—soit en superficie, soit en argent—le droit de propriété territoriale des Métis au titre de leur sang indien. Cette base, il la découvre enfin dans l'Acte du Manitoba, qui a consacré, selon lui, le principe selon lequel les Métis ont droit au 1/7 des terres.

En effet, il était stipulé dans l'Acte du Manitoba que les Métis recevraient 1,400,000 acres de terre. Or, comme le Manitoba avait une superficie totale de 9,000,000 acres, cela signifiait environ 1/7 des terres. Mais sur la base du recensement ultérieur, il fut accordé 240 acres de terrain à chaque Métis du Manitoba. Selon le gouvernement, cette portion de 240 acres était tout ce à quoi les Métis vivant au Manitoba ou hors du Manitoba avaient droit. Mais Riel argumente que "la base de la répartition a été la superficie du terrain et non la population". En conséquence, il maintient que la répartition des terres pour les Métis des Territoires du Nord-Ouest doit se faire selon la proportion du 1/7 de la superficie totale.

Dans son discours à la fin du procès, Riel justifie l'équitabilité de cette proportion de 1/7 des terres. En se basant sur le principe que la terre augmente de valeur quand elle est cultivée et que "les blancs par leur civilisation ont des moyens d'améliorer la terre que les sauvages et les métis n'ont pas", il affirme que les blancs, en venant "dans notre pays sauvage, sur notre terre inculte, pour nous aider de leur civilisation" ont droit de dire: votre terre "ne vaut aujourd'hui qu'un septième de ce qu'elle vaudra quand elle sera ouverte à la civilisation" (Canada, 1886:220-221).

Riel ne manque pas non plus de souligner que, aussi bien en Colombie Britannique que dans les provinces de l'est (Québec, Ontario, Maritimes), des Métis vivent méprisés sous le costume indien et qu'ils ont les mêmes droits à la propriété du sol de ces territoires que les Métis du Manitoba et du Nord-Ouest en ont sur leur sol.

Cependant, Riel en arrive alors à distinguer nettement le droit des Métis du droit des Indiens. Dans son discours à la fin de son procès, il affirme: "Pour les sauvages, ce ne sont pas les terres, c'est un septième du revenu à mesure qu'il augmentera'' (Canada, 1886:220). Rappelons-nous que, selon la synthèse antérieure de Riel, les Indiens n'existeront plus comme nation spécifique, puisqu'ils contribueront ainsi à métisser chacun de ces peuples. N'existant plus comme entité spécifique ils n'ont donc pas besoin de terre nationale. Pourtant Riel désire que, dans leur union avec les autres peuples, ils puissent apporter une sorte de dot. Cette dot sera constituée du septième des revenus que le gouvernement canadien tirera de la vente des terres. Evidemment, Riel tait, dans son discours au procès, cette idée du métissage global qui éliminera les Indiens.

c) L'utopie politico-religieuse
C'est sur la base de ce principe du droit des Métis au septième des terres que Riel reformule son utopie politoco-religieuse.

Riel affirme que, puisque le gouvernement canadien n'a pas donné aux Métis le 1/7 des terres du Nord-Ouest, ces derniers conservent leur droit de propriété sur tout le territoire du Nord-Ouest. Ils peuvent donc négocier la vente de leur territoire avec d'autres partenaires.

Dans un premier temps, Riel brandit la menace d'une invasion du Nord-Ouest par une ligue pluri-ethnique américaine à qui les Métis vendraient leur droit de propriété du Nord-Ouest, à la condition de pouvoir conserver un septième des terres. Dans quelques années, cette ligue serait assez puissante pour faire élire un président américain de son choix. Ce président lancerait ensuite les Etats-Unis à l'attaque de l'Amérique britannique du Nord, dans le but de permette à ces différents groupes ethniques d'entrer en possession des territoires acquis des Métis, pour fonder une nouvelle Irlande, une nouvelle Italie, une nouvelle Belgique, etc. (Lettre de Riel à Deane, Dewdney et Macdonald, 16 juillet 1885).

Par ailleurs, dans une pétition au président Cleveland des Etats-Unis, Riel lui demande carrément d'annexer le Nord-Ouest aux Etats-Unis, d'y introduire les institutions américaines et d'installer James W. Taylor comme gouverneur et lui, Riel, comme premier ministre et secrétaire (Lettre de Riel à Taylor pour le président Cleveland). A un autre moment, il propose au premier ministre Macdonald du Canada une mini-réalisation au Manitoba de son vaste projet d'immigration pluri-ethnique. Réalisation qu'il voudrait lui-même mettre en oeuvre sous l'autorité de Macdonald (Lettre de Riel à Macdonald, 16 juillet 1885).

Enfin, dans son discours à la fin de son procès, Riel distingue nettement deux moyens différents pour réaliser son projet de peuplement pluri-ethnique: 1- un moyen extrême et violent, soit la ligue des dix nations venant des Etats-Unis pour s'emparer du Nord-Ouest par la force, advenant le cas où le gouvernement canadien continuerait de refuser aux Métis leur 1/7 des terres; 2- un moyen pacifique et constitutionnel, soit l'installation de Riel au gouvernement d'Ottawa avec la responsabilité d'inviter directement de l'Europe ces diverses ethnies à venir s'installer dans le Nord-Ouest, advenant le cas évidemment où le gouvernement canadien accepterait de donner aux Métis leur 1/7 des terres (Canada, 1886:218-220).

Mais quelles sont ces dix nations que Riel veut voir s'installer dans le Nord-Ouest? C'est encore dans son discours à la fin de son procès qu'il est le plus explicite: (Canada, 1886:2l9-226). S'installeraient dans le Manitoba, les immigrants d'origine française et canadienne-française; s'installeraient dans le Nord-Ouest, les immigrants d'origine bavaroise, italienne, polonaise, irlandaise; s'installeraient de l'autre côté des Rocheuses, les immigrants d'origine danoise, suédoise, norvégienne, juive.

Remarquons enfin que ce projet politique baigne toujours dans une réflexion millénariste. Riel le relie à sa révélation sur la déchéance de l'Europe et de la papauté, due aux conséquences néfastes de la révolution française et de l'action du libéralisme. Le Nouveau-Monde qu'il veut fonder grâce à l'hospitalité du peuple métis deviendra le lieu béni de régénération pour quelques semences privilégiées des nations de l'Ancien-Monde; il deviendra aussi le lieu de régénération de la papauté catholique. Alors le feu de la guerre embrasera et détruira l'Europe (Lettre de Riel à Mgr Taché, 24 juillet 1885).

En somme, on décèle facilement à la source de cette vision utopique de Riel une conscience très vive des particularités ou des mentalités nationales ou ethniques qui dégénèrent souvent en oppositions, en discordes, en haines, en querelles et en guerres. Toute sa vie, Riel a connu, par expérience personnel, ce choc des mentalités et des cultures: lui, le Métis des Plaines, il a été éduqué en milieu canadien-français; au Manitoba, en 1869-70, il a échoué dans sa tentative de soulever une réaction unanime des Métis francophones et anglophones et, en même temps, il s'est heurté à l'opposition farouche des orangistes ontariens: il connut aussi de très près les difficultés d'adaptation des immigrés canadiens-français en Nouvelle-Angleterre; sa fréquentation de certains Irlandais catholiques d'allégeance fénienne l'a initié aux luttes de ces derniers avec les Anglais; au coeur de l'Ouest américain, il connut enfin les préjugées méprisants des Blancs contre les Indiens.

De ce constat dramatique est née son utopie politico-religieuse.

d) L'abjuration et l'orthodoxification de son message religieux
Au début d'août 1885, Riel, sous la pression des aumôniers assignés à la prison de Regina, signe une abjuration de toutes ses erreurs et hérésies. Il y renonce même à sa "fausse mission de prophète". Pourtant c'est le glaive au coeur qu'il signe. En fait, s'il accepte de renoncer à certaines de ses "hérésies", il ne peut se résoudre à renoncer à la mission prophétique qui lui a été confiée. Quelques jours plus tard, il a une vision de Mgr Bourget qui lui apparaît sous la forme d'un "soleil très resplendissant, mais dans ce soleil il y avait un chemin croche. Ce chemin croche, écrit-il au Père Cochin (11 août 1885), n'était autre chose que sa mission dans laquelle il avait changé d'opinion'', en

abjurant (Martel, 1976:580-590).

Dans les mois qui suivent, il s'efforce donc de ramener dans les limites de l'orthodoxie catholique romaine ses idées de réformes religieuses, tout en conservant sa conviction d'avoir à remplir aussi une mission prophétique (Martel, 1976:602-60).

Enfin, il s'efforce de justifier sa mission prophétique en affirmant qu'elle consiste à "élucider les Ecritures", à "expliquer l'essence de Dieu et de l'âme humaine", à "expliquer le plan de la création elle-même, comme Dieu le lui a révélé", comme Riel l'écrit à Jukes, médecin de la prison de Regina.

En somme, son rôle de prophète consiste à fournir une explication de caractère logique et même "scientifique" de la révélation biblique et de la doctrine catholique qui les rendraient plausibles aux yeux des hommes modernes.

Enfin, il lui appartient aussi en tant que prophète d'annoncer les grandes lignes de la destinée des nations et de supputer la chronologie des "derniers temps" (Martel, 1976:604-614).

Conclusion

On doit donc conclure que Riel ne semble pas avoir tiré toutes les conséquences du mythe de l'origine hébraïque des Indiens de l'Amérique de Nord. On a même l'impression qu'il s'agit là d'un bloc erratique dans la chaine de ses réflexions. Ainsi, il n'affirme jamais explicitement que le "retour" des Indiens-Hébreux au sein du Peuple Elu est une condition essentielle à l'avènement du Royaume de Dieu. Il n'affirme pas non plus que la mission messianique du peuple métis lui vient de son ascendance hébraïque, au contraire, il cherche les les antécédents de cette mission du côté de l'ascendance française des Métis, lui-même se disant un descendant du roi saint Louis par sa mère. En d'autres mots, le sang indien, dans sa pensée messianique ne remplit que deux fonctions subsidiares: premièrement, il assure aux Métis un droit inaliénable à la possession du sol de la nouvelle Terre Promise; et, deuxièmement, le sang indien, en se mêlant aux sangs des diverses nations appelées à peupler le Nouveau-Monde, les réunira en une large fraternité et leur permettra de participer ainsi aux bienfaits messianiques de la nation *métisse canadienne-française* seule dépositaire des promesses divines par son ascendance française et catholique.

En ce sens, il est permis de dire que la pensée messianique de Riel n'est pas à proprement parler du type "nativiste", puisqu'elle ne postule pas un "retour à des moeurs primitives", v.g. indiennes. En effet, Riel ne propose jamais à son peuple l'adoption de moeurs ou de coutumes typiquement indiennes.

Le problème majeur auquel il s'attaque est celui de la *diversité antagoniste* entre les peuples. Mais il n'en cherche pas la solution dans un retour en arrière: il ne songe pas à isoler son peuple dans un ghetto pour protéger ses traits distinctifs et ancestraux. Au contraire, il cherce la solution à cette diversité antagoniste dans un mouvement de large ouverture. De large ouverture, mais jusqu'à une certaine limite. En effet, l'idéal de Riel n'est pas celui de "melting pot" qui veut fondre ensemble les diversités ethniques pour créer *une* nouvelle nation. Ce qu'il entrevoit, annonce et espère c'est une unité *dans la diversité:* chacun des peuples conservant les principaux traits de sa spécificité, mais contenus dans des institutions politiques, sociales et religieuses destinées à les harmoniser.

Ce problème auquel Riel eut à se confronter est-il tellement différent du problème qui secoue le Canada et même le monde d'aujourd'hui? Riel, dans un effort de réflexion mystico-politique, a refusé à la fois l'assimilation et le "melting" pour chercher une solution du côté d'une *conféderétion de nations métissées.* Sa solution aurait-elle pu avoir quelque chance de survie...et à quelles conditions? Enfin, pouvons-nous encore nous demander: existe-t-il beaucoup d'autres solutions logiques et raisonnables à ce problème, en dehors de toute espérance messianique?

En terminant la rédaction de ce texte, je tombe sur un article de journal intitulé: "Le grand chef des Métis propose une conférence des nations".(Le Devoir, 21 août 1978:3). Harry Daniels, chef des Métis du Canada, s'adresse aux 230 délégués de l'*Alliance laurentienne des Métis et Indiens sans statut du Québec.* "Personne d'autre au Canada, affirme Harry Daniels, ne représente mieux que les Métis la fusion du vieux continent et du nouveau monde". Il poursuit en "réclamant la fondation d'une conférence nationale des différents peuples formant la mosaïque canadienne". Il ajoute que "la réalité métisse, et non pas celle des francophones ou des anglophones, constitue la véritable base de la culture canadienne". A son avis, "la communauté métisse de l'ouest constituait un véritable embryon de culture canadienne. Mais cette identité a été niée et refoulée par un gouvernement central qui préférait chercher en Angleterre plutôt que sur son propre sol sa définition de la culture".

Il est vrai que le problème auquel a été confronté Riel n'a pas trouvé sa solution! Mais on aimerait savoir si Monsieur Daniels voit l'*embryon de culture canadienne métisse* comme l'effet d'une action de "melting pot", créant une nouvelle culture, ou plutôt comme une certaine harmonisation des cultures dans le respect de leurs diversités?

Bibliographie

1. *Sources manuscrites,* Pour une description assez compléte des *archives Riel,* voir MARTEL, 1976:640-685.
2   *Sources Imprimées.*

BOTKIN, Alex. C., 1900: "The John Brown of the Half-Breeds", *Rocky Mountain Magazine,* 1 (1):18-22.

CANADA, Département du secrétariat d'Etat, 1886: *Epitome des documents parlementaires relatifs à la rébellion du Nord-Quest, 1885.* Maclean, Roger & Co., par ordre du Parlement, Ottawa, 392 p (Trad. française du procès de Riel, pp. 14-227).

CHAMPAGNE, Antoine, c.r.i.c., 1969: "La famille de Louis Riel, notes généalogiques et historiques." *Mémoires de la Société généalogique canadienne-française, XX (3).*

FLANAGAN, Thomas E., 1974 a: "Louis 'David' Riel: prophet, priestking, infallible pontiff." *Journal of Canadian Studies/Revue d'Etudes Canadiennes,* pp. 15-26.

———1974 b: "Louis Riel's Religious Beliefs: A Letter to Bishop Taché", *Saskatchewan History,* XXVII (1):15-28.

———1974 c: "A New View of Louis Riel"; in Richard Allen (ed.) *Religion and Society in the Prairie West,* Regina, Canadian Plains Studies, III:35-52.

———1975 a: "Louis Riel: Insanity ànd Prophecy." *CALUM: The Alumni Association of the University of Calgary,* Calgary, Alberta, 6 (3): 4,5,8,9.

———1975 b: "The Mission of Louis Riel." *Alberta History,* 23 (1): 1-12.

———1975 c: "The Religion of Louis Riel." *The Quarterly of Canadian Studies for the Secondary School,* 4 (1): 3-14.

———1976: *The Diaries of Louis Riel,* Hurtig Publishers, Edmonton, 187 p.

———1978: *Louis 'David' Riel: Prophet of the New World.* Sous presse.

GIRAUD, Marcel, 1945: *Le Métis canadien. Son rôle dan l'historie des provinces de l'Ouest.* Institut d'ethnologie, Paris, LVI + 1296 p.

HOWARD, Joseph Kinsey, 1970: *The Strange Empire of Louis Riel.* Swan Publishing Co. Ltd., Toronto 2nd ed., 480 p.

MARTEL, Gilles, 1972: *Louis Riel, les années de formation.* Mémoire de maîtrise en sciences humanies des religions, Université de Sherbrook, 284 p.

———1976: *Le messianisme de Louis Riel (1844-1885).* Sherbrooke/Paris: non publié, 711 p. (Thèse de doctorat en sociologie présentée à l'Ecole des Hautes Etudes en Sciences Sociales, France).

———1977: "Louis Riel: ferveur nationaliste et foi religieuse." *Relations,* 37 (425): 103-105.

MARTEL, Gilles, CAMPBELL Glen, FLANAGAN, Thomas E., 1977: *Louis Riel, poésies de jeunesse.* les Editions du Blé, St. Boniface, X + 161 p.

MORTON, W.L. (ed.), 1956: *Alexander Begg's Red River Journal and other Papers.* (Introduction by MORTON, W.L., pp. 1-148). Champlain Society, Toronto, 635 p.

MORTON, W.L., *Manitoba, A History.* University of Toronto Press, Toronto, XIII + 547 p.

MULVANEY, Charles Pelham, 1885: *The History of the North-West Rebellion of 1885.* A.H. Hovey & Co., Toronto, 424 p., front illust. (incl. ports., maps).

NADEAU, Gabriel, 1944: "La folie de Riel." *Le Devoir,* XXXV (248), 27 octobre 1944, complet rendu. Conférence à la société historique de Montréal, le 25 octobre 1944.) (Le texte complet se trouve dans la collection Nadeau de la Bibliothèque Nationale du Québec, Montréal).

O'DEA, Thomas F., 1968: *The Mormons.* The University of Chicago Press, Chicago/London 6th ed., (c. 1957), XII + 289 p.

OSLER, E.B., 1962: *Louis Riel: un homme à prendre.* Ed. du Jour, Montréal, 299 p. (Trad. Vien, Rossel).

SMITH, J., (trad.), 1965: *Le Livre de Mormon.* Récit écrit sur plaques, de la main de Mormon d'après les plaques de Néphi. Traduit en anglais, d'après les plaques, par Joseph Smith, fils. Publié par l'Eglise de Jésus-Christ des Saints des Derniers Jours, 6e éd. française, 530 p.

STANELY, G.F.G., 1966: *The Birth of Western Canada. A History of the Riel Rebellions.* University of Toronto Press, Toronto, XIV + 475 p.

————1969: *Louis Riel,* Ryerson Press, Toronto, 5th ed., (c 1963), 433 p.

THOMAS, Lewis H., 1970: "Document of Western History, Louis Riel's Petition of Rights, 1884." *Saskatchewan History,* XXIII (1): 16-26.

XXXXX, 1887: *Le véritable Riel, tel que dépeint dans les lettres de Sa Grandeur Mgr Grandin, évêque de St-Albert, du Rév. P. Leduc, vicaire général de St-Albert, du Rév. P. André, supérieur des missions du district de Carleton, des Rév. Pères Touze, Fourmond, Vegreville, Moulin et Lecoq, missionnaires du Nord Ouest, d'une religieuse de Batoche, etc. Suivi d'extraits des mandements de Nos Seigneurs les évêques, concernant l'agitation Riel.* Imprimerie générale, Montréal, 63p.

3

Louis Riel's Name "David"

Thomas Flanagan

A LOOK INTO the card catalogue of any sizeable Canadian library, will reveal a number of entries under the heading RIEL, LOUIS DAVID. One will probably not wonder whether this was the man's true name, since librarians have a reputation for accuracy. But in fact his name was only Louis Riel; he did not begin to call himself David until he was more than thirty years old; and when he did, he almost always put the new name in inverted commas—Louis "David" Riel—to show that it had a special significance. The story of how he acquired that name and what it meant to him is worth telling because it casts a little light on the inner world of this strange man.

Riel was born and baptized on October 22 or 23, 1844. The former date comes from his mother, the latter from himself.[1] We shall probably never know which is correct, for the baptismal registry of St. Boniface was subsequently destroyed by fire. That loss also means we shall probably never discover what Riel's full baptismal name was. He was never called anything other than Louis, as far as we know; but there is reason to think he bore additional names. When he was about twenty and had recently been expelled from the College of Montreal, he wrote three letters to George-Etienne Cartier asking for help in finding a job.[2] He signed them J.B.A. Louis Riel. The "A" is a mystery. The J.B. probably stood for Jean-Baptiste; Riel had several ancestors by that name, his father's name was Jean-Louis, and he named his own son Jean. But nowhere is there a trace of David.

The name first appeared in Riel's life in October, 1873. Because Cartier died in the spring of that year, there had to be a by-election to fill his seat in the

House of Commons. He had represented the Manitoba riding of Provencher because Riel, who could easily have won it in the previous general election, had stepped aside in Cartier's behalf. Now Riel decided to contest the by-election. In the midst of the campaign, a group of Canadians in Winnipeg succeeded in getting a warrant sworn out for Riel's arrest for the murder of Thomas Scott. Riel went into hiding in the woods at Vermette's Point across the Red River from St. Norbert. He had been there a month when he was unanimously elected *in absentia* on October 13, 1873.[3]

There are two explanations of how these circumstances led to the appearance of the name David. Let us consider the more prosaic one first. Riel was now a fugitive. Somehow he had to travel east without being arrested. His friend Joseph Dubuc wrote to him on October 17, advising him to adopt an alias: "In hotels and on steamboats you will be more or less obliged to give a name. And it would not be prudent to use your own. So take some name. A very ordinary name like Pierre *David* or Jean Dubois has been suggested. (Italics added)".[4] It is not known whether Riel travelled east under the pseudonym of David, but there is evidence that he used it in Montreal in January, 1874.[5]

The second explanation is more poetic. When Dubuc visited Riel in hiding, he compared him to the David of the ancient Hebrews.[6] The point of similarity of course, was that Riel, like David, had achieved an unexpected success as a young man. Each had defeated an external power which threatened his people with destruction. And then each, in a sudden reversal of fortune, had been compelled to flee: David from the wrath of Saul, Riel from Canadian justice.

The story is plausible enough. A comparison with David is the sort of remark that Dubuc could easily have made to Riel. Both knew their Bible thoroughly after their years at the College of Montreal. But there is no contemporary documentation of the story. It did not get written down until many years later, when Riel was already convinced of being "the David of the Christian era". Hence we cannot be sure whether Riel's association with the name David began in this appropriately symbolic fashion, or whether it was merely an alias to avoid detection.

For the next two years there is no record of the name David in Riel's life. In April of 1874, when he made his dramatic foray into the House of Commons to sign the Members' register, he used the simple signature Louis Riel.[7] The same will be found on all his correspondence of the period. Yet it seems likely that he was internally meditating upon his resemblance with David and finding consolation in it.

For these were very difficult years for Riel. He suffered one political setback after another, culminating in the amnesty of April 1875, which sentenced him to five years of banishment from Canada. He went to Washington, D.C. to ask President Grant to help him mount an invasion of Manitoba but that plan came to nothing.[8]

As politics disappointed him, Riel turned more and more to religion. He began to think that his hardships were a purification and preparation for a greater mission. The downtrodden Métis would be a new chosen people; and he, at their head, would lead a tremendous religious revival in America. He would be a prophet, the "Prophet of the New World".[9]

He began to have ecstatic and visionary experiences in December, 1875, while staying in Washington, D.C., with a friend, Edmond Mallet. He also began to speak openly and very excitedly about his divine mission. Mallet, thinking Riel had gone insane, took him to stay with Father Primeau in Worcester, Massachusetts. Riel was then passed from hand to hand until he ended in the care of his uncle and aunt, John and Lucie Lee, who lived near Montreal. After several weeks of trying to cope with their nephew, they committed him—without obtaining or seeking his consent—to the lunatic asylum of Saint-Jean-de-Dieu in Longue-Pointe, a suburb of Montreal. It was March 6, 1876.

At this point the name David appears in the story again. Riel's relatives, and the friends with whom they were co-operating, did not want his true identity to be widely known at the hospital. He was supposed to be in exile, so his presence in the country was illegal and would have caused a scandal if publicized. Thus a pseudonym was employed. Riel was admitted to the asylum as Louis R. David.[10] Although it cannot be proven from the documents, the choice of David under these circumstances suggests that Riel had been using that alias with the knowledge of his friends.

Before Riel was admitted, his uncle had an interview with Dr. Henry Howard, visiting physician at the hospital. Dr. Howard was appointed by the provincial government as a sort of inspector of the asylum. Hence it was necessary to gain his co-operation if Riel was to be secretly admitted. Lee rather reluctantly revealed his nephew's true identity to Howard, who "consented immediately with pleasure to the idea of admitting Louis David Riel to the asylum the next day under the name of Louis R. David, and promised to do all (he) could to keep it a secret from the nuns, the orderlies and strangers. . ."[11]

This conspiracy caused an unpleasant incident when Riel was brought to the hospital. In Dr. Howard's words:

> I said to him: "I am happy to meet you, Mr. David; I am Dr. Howard." He made a gesture of surprise and cried: "Why do you call me 'David'? My name is Louis David Riel." Taking a little prayer book from his pocket, and opening it to the first page, he gave it to me and said: "See my name there, Louis David Riel, written in the hand of my beloved sister."[12]

At once the Sister who was present grabbed the book, ripped out the offending page, and said, "You are known here only under the name of Monsieur

David!'' A terrible struggle ensued, and Dr. Howard recalled that he had never seen a man in such fury. If Riel had not been restrained, he would have attacked the nun and '' torn her to pieces.''[13]

If Dr. Howard's memory can be trusted (the story was not written down until a decade later), Riel had assumed the identity of Louis ''David'' Riel by the time he entered the hospital. In any case, the name became enormously important to Riel within a few weeks.

He explained its meaning to Bishop Ignace Bourget in a long letter written in two instalments on April 20 and May 1, 1876. He referred to his concealment under a false identity at the hospital when he wrote:

> It is your enemies (God said to Riel) whom I have used to make you resemble David (by compelling him to flee for his life) and your so-called friends whom I am using to make you have the name of David (by using a false name at the asylum).[14]

Although Riel did not spell it out, he probably remembered that David had also been taken for a madman at the court of the Phoenicians, where he had gone to hide from Saul. The difference was that David had intentionally pretended to be insane, whereas Riel was an involuntary patient in the asylum. But in later years, perhaps inspired by David's example, Riel would claim that he had purposely simulated madness so the Canadian government would stop persecuting the Métis.[15]

Riel's imaginative mind now began to see resemblances to David going far beyond the situation of flight and concealment. He elaborated a number of similarities which carry us deep into the private world of his revelations.

He had learned from God that the North American Indians were really descendants of certain ancient Hebrews who had crossed the ocean in search of freedom. The Métis, the chosen people of the present age, were thus affiliated with the first chosen people, the Jews, through the Indians. This led Riel to discover an ingenious genealogical resemblance between himself and David. David had been seven-eights Hebrew and one-eigth Moabite. His paternal great-grandmother Ruth was from Moab. Riel, in comparison was seven-eigths French-Canadian and one-eigth Indian, or Hebrew. His paternal grandmother was a Chipewayan woman, making his genealogy a mirror image of David's. God said to him:

> By the Indian blood which flows in your veins, you are Jewish. And through your paternal great-grandmother you belong to the Jewish nation as much as the first David belonged to the Gentiles, through his paternal great-grandmother. And as the first David belonged to the Jewish nation through all his other ancestors, so you belong to the Gentiles through all your other ancestors. You are the David of the Christian era, of who the former David was only the symbol.[16]

To be the "David of the Christian era" was not merely an empty title. Riel interpreted it quite literally. He wrote that he would be the "messiah of human glory whom the people of Jacob expected to find in the incarnate world."[17] The Jews had rejected Christ because He had been a spiritual messiah. Riel would lead them to Christ by founding the earthly kingdom they had always expected. God told him:

> You will re-establish the people which is dear to me (Jews) . . . A third of the Hebrew people is going to be converted now. Through the triumphant and victorious Henry V (the Comte de Chambord, Bourbon pretender to the French throne), you will give Poland to the House of Jacob, so that on its soil I may once again gaze upon the throne of David.[18]

On May 19, 1876, Riel was transferred to the asylum of Saint-Michel-Archange at Beauport, outside Quebec City. He was registered once again under the alias of Louis R. David (a new alias, Larochelle, was also employed at Beauport).[19] Riel continued to cling to his identification with the Biblical David. While at Beauport, he worked out the details of a vast reform of Christianity. As the modern David, he would reintroduce important elements of Judaism into religious practice: The Mosaic Law, circumcision, polygamy, the Saturday sabbath. The result of this system, had it ever been established, would have been a form of Judaeo-Christianity something like that practised by the earliest followers of Christ before St. Paul released them from the Old Law.[20]

One curious element in the program was incest. Riel wrote that marriage between brother and sister would be permitted, even encouraged, under certain circumstances—chiefly if the death of a father meant that his oldest son had to devote himself to caring for his mother and younger children, thus making it impossible to marry in the conventional way. Riel could not have been directly imitating Jewish models, since incest was sternly forbidden by the Mosaic Law (although it seems to have been practised in patriarchal times). However, Riel may have been indirectly inspired by the Hebrew practice of "levirate marriage", that is the marriage of a man to his brother's widow in order to protect family property. Riel adduced similar utilitarian reasons to defend his proposal for incest.

Personal motives may also have played a role. The circumstances which, in Riel's view, justified incest were precisely those of his own youth. His father died when he was nineteeen, leaving a numerous family of younger children to be cared for. Riel may have had an incestuous desire for his sister Sara, although the evidence on this score is tenuous at best.[21]

There is an interesting connection between incest and the family of David, whose son Ammon, raped his half-sister Thamar. David's failure to punish this crime led Thamar's brother Absalom to take his own revenge; such was the beginning of the dissolution of David's family. Now Riel, after he had been discharged from Beauport and had become secretly engaged to Evelina Barnabé, wrote a poem to her about this subject.

> Et tout à vénérer que soit le sanctuaire
> De la famille, hélas, il se trouve souillé
> Plus souvent qu'on voudrait, même entre soeur et frère
> Excusez la parole claire
> Car je ne vous tiens pas un discours embrouillé
> Et se jamais Dieu veut que vous deveniz mère
> Evelina, souvenez-vous
> Que le fils de David, Ammon, commit l'inceste
> Avec sa soeur Thamara. Et le divin courroux
> S'alluma pour punir ce désordre funeste.[22]

Perhaps contemplation of the sad fate of David's family helped Riel to overcome his desire for incest. At any rate, he only advocated the idea once in all his writings.[23] We do not know if he repudiated it, since he wrote no more about it, except in the poem to Evelina; but incest certainly does not appear in a favourable light there.

Incest aside, Riel's intention was to revive certain elements of Judaism and fuse them with Catholicism. Thus his religion was more than Judaism, and he was more than David. He signed his Name "Louis 'David' Riel: Prophet, Priest-King, Infallible Pontiff."[24] Certainly "infallible pontiff" was a Christian concept of which the Jews had no inkling. Yet the other titles were Davidic. As the Jews had not divided church and state, David had been priest as well as king; and his prophetic voice had spoken in the psalms. Riel's identity as a new David meant that he aspired to gather all power, both temporal and spiritual, into his own hands, and wield it under the divine inspiration vouchsafed to prophets.

This theocratic program was worthy of the millennium, and indeed Riel understood himself as the harbinger of Christ's return to earth. He applied to himself the predictions of the Book of the Apocalypse. He became the knight on the white horse. (6:1-2)

> The Apocalypse is a trustworthy guide which I have never understood. But now I can explain its parables and its divine numbers. The Lord Jesus Christ tells me: Louis, you are Louis: you are the knight to whom I give my white horse of the Apocalypse . . .
> David, you are David: you will chant the psalms of my glory till the end. Your throne is established for ever . . .
> Riel, you are Riel: I will give you strength of body and soul against the spiritual and temporal enemies of my catholic, apostolic, and living church of the Shining Mountains.[25]

Riel's religious enthusiasm was most intense in 1876. The following year it subsided somewhat, at least to external appearances. He no longer insisted that others acknowledge the validity of his mission as the modern David. It is not clear whether this was a genuine change of heart, or merely learning to say what was expected of him—perhaps a little of both. At any rate, he was released from the Asylum of Beauport on January 23, 1878, and returned to the United States.

There now ensued a most interesting period in Riel's life. If he had ever truly given up his novel beliefs, they quickly returned in full force. He was having visions and revelations within months of his release from the hospital.[26] Yet he kept this side of his life private. He was neither insane nor heretical to all external appearances. The prophet-king was in hiding. He determined to remain inconspicuous until God Himself would show the way by performing some extraordinary and highly visible miracle on his behalf. Then it would be time to convert the world to his new cult.

Although he kept his secret well, he occasionally confided, at least partially, in sympathetic friends. Around 1881 he told James Willard Schultz, a Montana trader:

> Do you know, these people of mine are just as were the children of Israel, a persecuted race deprived of their heritage. But I will redress their wrongs; I will wrest justice for them from the tyrant. I will be unto them a second David.[27]

Like David, he too composed psalms, which he wrote out at night by the light of the fire in the Métis encampments. But these disclosures were exceptional. Riel took pains to appear "normal" in the eyes of most observers.

The name David, however, was obviously still important to him. He pursued the interesting strategy of trying to get official approval for it. He had already taken steps in that direction in Beauport when he had written to Bishop Taché explaining that he had particularly asked for help of the "Holy King David" during the troubles in Red River. He had promised David that if the latter would defend him, he would one day definitely place himself under his patronage by taking his name. He aske Taché:

> Deign to bless me in Jesus and Mary, and confirm my second Baptismal name, the name of a great servant of God, that I may have the grace of signing Louis "David" Riel.[28]

Taché's reply is not recorded, but we can assume he gave Riel no encouragement.

On March 9, 1882, Riel's common-law marriage was blessed by a Jesuit missionary in Montana. With the permission of the priest, Louis went through the ceremony as Louis "David" Riel, and inscribed his adopted name on the wedding certificate.[29] He similarly used the name David on his naturalization papers when he became an American citizen on March 16, 1883.[30] He drafted a letter to Taché telling of his marriage and change of citizenship and pointing out how he had used his adopted name. The implication was that he was officially recognized as "David" in the United States, even without Taché's approval. But the letter was probably never sent.[31]

Riel finally emerged from spiritual seclusion during the North-West Rebellion. That movement was as much a religious as a political event. Riel introduced the Métis to a modified version of the creed which he had propounded at Beauport. He declared that Rome had fallen and that religious primacy had passed to the Métis. Although he was silent about some of his more extreme ideas, such as polygamy, he impressed upon the Métis that they were a new chosen people who should adopt the practices of Judaism. He went as far as instituting the Saturday sabbath through a resolution of the Exovedate. And of course he made no secret of his affiliation with David. He boldly signed official papers "Louis 'David' Riel, Exovede."[32]

As General Middleton's army drew inexorably towards Batoche, Riel once again imagined himself in the role of the youthful David, saving his people from certain defeat. He wrote in his diary:

> I have seen the giant; he is coming, he is hideous. It is Goliath. . . Because he will not humble himself, his head is cut off.[33]

But the aging David was not equal to the task. This time Goliath was the victor, and Riel surrendered, after the Métis were overwhelmed in the battle of Batoche. He was brought to Regina, where he was tried and convicted of high treason.

Once again Riel took consolation in the story of David. At his trial he told the jury that he had been "hunted as an elk for fifteen years," ever since Wolseley's troops had entered Red River in August, 1870. But by Riel's own computations, David had had to spend seventeen years in the wilderness before assuming the throne of Saul. His own deliverance thus could not be too far away. "If the misfortunes that I have had to go through were to be as long as those of old David, I would have two years still, but I hope it will come sooner."[34]

When these words were spoken on August 1, 1885, Riel had been convicted but not yet sentenced. The imposition of the death sentence broke his confidence, temporarily at least. Fathers Cochin and Fourmond, taking advantage of this weakness, persuaded him to sign a recantation of all his heresies and of his "false mission as prophet," the root of all his errors. Riel signed, and thus re-entered the Church on August 5. Yet it is doubtful whether this abjuration was really sincere. Within a few days he would again be receiving revelations from the Holy Ghost. Even when he signed the document, he made his own copy which he headed Louis "David" Riel, not Louis Riel, as the priests had done.[35] It could perhaps be interpreted, under the circumstances, as a small gesture of defiance and belief in his mission.

Riel now had only about three months to live. He remained within the Church, but only through the forbearance of his confessor, Father André; for he continued to experience revelations and to assert his prophetic mission. He freely used the signature Louis "David" Riel in these last months. And, as the following diary entry shows, he still saw himself as the valiant young champion of a small people facing the giant of oppression. Soon he wrote,

(t)he spouse of Christ, the Church, my mother, will shower me with her own blessings. Her solicitude will honour me because I, little David in the service of the great King, had the courage to go outside the camp of Israel for a moment, to try to hold off the giant who was marching against all of us with his redoubtable strength and reputation. [36]

What shall we make of Riel's identification with David? First, note that it was not a case of schizophrenic change of identity. Riel never asserted that he literally was David, neither the original nor a reincarnation. He was always aware that the association with David was metaphorical, which he emphasized by writing his adopted name in quotation marks.

He made David's career the model of his own, just as he made the Hebrews at large the model of the new chosen people, the Métis. David's life resembled, in miniature, the history of the Hebrews as conceived by their prophets: the initial success, a period of suffering, and a glorious final salvation.

Thus Riel found in the Bible a symbolic explanation of his own life and the history of his people. The analogy grew into the new religion which Riel intended to found, a blend of Judaism and Catholicism with a special role for the Métis. As a would-be religious founder, Riel has many parallels among other leaders of native peoples who have led their followers in revolt not only against the white man's government but against his Church. Religion can be as much a weapon as guns or swords. In its own way, the Bible has sparked more resistance movements among colonized nations than have Marx or Lenin.[37]

4

Some Comments on the Social Origins of the Riel Protest of 1869

Fritz Pannekoek

THE ENGLIGH-SPEAKING folk of Red River looked with excitement and hope on the debates that surrounded the confederation of the eastern provinces. The Protestant Canadians, arriving in vocal and visible numbers in the 1860s to farm along the Assiniboine and to trade in the small village of Winnipeg, provided ample evidence of the vigour that the new connection would bring. All were anxious that union be effected quickly and quietly. Even the Protestant English speaking mixed-bloods looked to Canada to pull Red River out of its morass of pettiness and squalor. When it became clear that Canada had secured the chartered land of the Hudson's Bay Company, most were ready, indeed anxious, to welcome the Canadian Governor, no matter how obnoxious he might be.

If the English-speaking half-breeds applauded the demise of old Red River with its peasant ways and too dominant patriarchs, the Catholic French-speaking Métis feared its passing. It was increasingly obvious as the 1860s piled drought upon locust plague, that the hunt, the fisheries, the freight boat, and the cart would provide only the most meagre subsistence. The Métis merchants also feared that union with Canada, with its inevitable railroads and high tariffs, would spell the end to the profitable creaking cart trains to St. Paul and the Saskatchewan country. Equally important, union with Canada would mean a Protestant supremacy. The attacks on the Catholic faith by Red River Protestants in the 1860s had taught the Métis that Protestantism was the devil incarnate. The bigots of that faith sought to discredit the Catholic Church, their morals and their lifestyles, and the Canadians who invaded the settlement in the later 1860s confirmed the fears of the Métis. The Canadian Governor-designate of the settlement was rumoured to have hanged at least two priests.

To the Métis hunters who wintered on the Saskatchewan plains, the debates that raged in Red River from the later fifties onward over the future of the North-West must have seemed irrelevant. It was their perception that the Company's despised and indifferent rule was finally at an end. Not all hated the Company with equal passion, but most recognized that the Company of 1869 was not the Company of legend. The great Chief Factors and greater Governors who had established the Company's reputation in the first instance had been replaced by a less inspired and more callous lot, and the decade of the 1860s saw mutiny after mutiny among the Métis manning the freight boats. The northern brigades were brought to virtual collapse and to the boatmen the insurrection in 1869 would be seen as the most successful mutiny of them all.

Each of the major groups that comprised Red River, then, had separate fears and unique motives for their involvement in the struggles of 1869. For the English-speaking mixed-bloods, it was a constitutional conflict gone away. From the 1850s onward, they applied pressure for a negotiated constitutional solution to the ills of Red River and its western hinterland. But then, when they were overwhelmed by the Métis initiatives, they resorted to military action if only to reaffirm the constitutional course. To the Red River Métis, however, 1869 was a defensive reaction arising out of their fear of the threat posed by a Protestant Canadian religious and economic supremacy; and to the Métis boatmen and winterers, outside the colony, 1869 was the high point of a decade of protest.

The English-speaking of the settlement had wanted union with Canada as early as 1856. William Kennedy, an embittered ex-Company man, who had spent a number of years in the east, returned to the settlement that year to spearhead an annexation movement. Throughout the winter of 1856-57 meetings were held in the English-speaking parishes. By spring, Kennedy, who many thought to be a secret agent of the Canadian Government, had manipulated the election of five members, including himself, to the Canadian legislature. The new members were already en route when news of Captain John Palliser's imminent arrival reached the settlement. It was thought then he had been empowered to negotiate the colony's future, and the five were recall-ed;[1] but Red River was to be disappointed in its hopes.

During this upheaval, the situation in the colony became exceedingly acrimonious when the pro-Canada movement split into a faction advocating crown colony status instead. Since crown colonies were not responsible for the salaries of their governors or the expenses of the military, many considered this to be the cheaper course. In the end, these arguments won out and the English-speaking united in 1862 to form a movement in favour of the crown colony option, particularly since the Canadian legislature seemed to ignore their every petition.

The head of the crown colony movement was the Rev. G. O. Corbett, a rather popular clergyman of the Church of England, who lived in Headingly. In 1862, Corbett was accused of attempting to perform an abortion on his maid servant, pregnant with his child, and the English-speaking mixed-bloods im-mediately assumed that it was a Company conspiracy to discredit the crown colony movement. When Corbett was found guilty and jailed, his supporters rioted. Corbett was reluctantly set free and the ringleaders of the riot jailed. Again the English-speaking mixed-blood horsemen rode to the jail to force the release of their brothers.[2] The situation had so deteriorated, and so little faith in the Company or in the Imperial Government remained, that the people of St. James and Headingly declared a "Provisional Government" in May 1863.[3] These parishes, along with Portage la Prairie, originally intended to secede from Red River and to form an independent colony subordinate only to the crown, but their original enthusiasm must have waned. What actually happen-ed to the provisional government is not known;' however, since it did not in-terfere with commerce or the government of the Upper Fort it was probably ignored, functioning in the end as little more than a parish council.

Whatever the outcome of the agitation of the 1860s, it is clear that the English-speaking half of the settlement was determined to effect a new political arrangement either within the Canadian union or as a crown colony. When news of the confederation movement in the Canadas drifted out to Red River in 1866, the English-speaking of the settlement seized the opportunity to negotiate with the colonies. As early as November, thirty-two of the settle-ment's most prominent settlers including Alexander Ross, Norman Kitson, Angus McBeth, John Pritchard and William Drever requested a public meeting to discuss the subject. On December 12, 1866, after much debate a petition with two hundred signatures pleading for union, was sent to the Im-perial Government. It would not even be acknowledged until July 18.[4]

The movement's principal leader appeared to be Thomas Spence, an English born storekeeper residing in Portage la Prairie, later to become clerk of the Manitoba legislature. He cultivated his Ontario contacts like Toronto M. P. Angus Morrison, in order to generate an interest in the Red River-Canadian union.[5] But there was little enthusiasm in Canada. Who was Thomas Spence and what and where was Red River? All the colony could do, and this was the advice from their Canadian sympathizers, was wait.

Events in Portage, a relatively isolated community with no real government of its own, pressed for more immediate and precipitious action. Riot and murder threatened to take over the settlement unless some form of government was imposed and in January 1868 the settlement resolved to proceed with the formation of yet another provisional government. A revenue tax was imposed and a jail was constructed. The new government's self-declared jurisdiction went from the 51st to the 49th parallels and from longitude 100 to the boundary of the Colony of Assiniboia. Thomas Spence served as the first President of the "Council of Manitoba," and was succeeded after the first year by a Mr. Curtis, who retained the position until the Riel interlude.

The Portage provisional government continued to press for recognition and Canadian union and while the English-speaking at Red River had developed cold feet, Portage chose to involve them in the scheme. In correspondence with the Imperial Government, Spence suggested that the Governor of Assiniboia, William Mactavish, be appointed the first Lieutenant-Governor of the new territory.[7] This only prompted the Imperial authorities to chastise the Portage clique for its illegal usurpation of power.[8] Nevertheless the president and his council were so anxious for union that they continued to press Lord Monck, the Canadian Governor General, and Sir John A. Macdonald for action, albeit without any degree of success.[9] To most in Ottawa, Spence and Manitoba were the ludicrous accidents of an anachronistic frontier. They could be ignored until such time as they became useful.

The initial pressure for negotiating a union with Canada, then ,came from the English-speaking mixed bloods and white settlers at Portage la Prairie and Red River. They preferred to press for orderly constitutional change, and turned to the creation of provisional governments only in frustration. Given their fervent desire for union, the armed resistance of the Métis in 1869 must have seemed sheer madness. But if it was insanity, it was criminal insanity and it would have to be opposed vigorously and if need be with violence.

When Riel stopped the surveys, formed a National Committee, barred the highway to St. Norbert and seized Upper Fort Garry, the English mixed-bloods were prepared to resist. They did so because they thought the union with Canada might be delayed again or that a new Métis-directed union might not be of their liking. In November and December of 1869 the mixed-bloods of St. Andrew's and St. Paul's had reached a decision—to retake the Upper Fort. By December 4 at least four hundred were ready to march. A lack of arms, ineffectual leadership and a reluctant Protestant clergy, as well as an indication by Riel that he would attempt a "constitutional" solution to the impasse with Canada, ended the crisis.

Again in February 1870 the English half-breeds, this time the Portage la

Prairie crowd spurred on by Canadians like Charles Mair, and the St. Andrew's group pushed by Jonn C. Schultz, decided to bring about union with Canada by force. On February 10, sixty men left Portage and joined four hundred recruits from the lower settlements of St. Andrew's and St. Paul's four days later. The plan was to meet at Kildonan, seize St. Boniface, and bombard the Upper Fort. Again because of lack of weapons, ideas, and leadership, the movement failed. The English half-breeds were forced to negotiate over their demands for territorial governments and minimal taxation with the Riel faction who would obviously control the union deliberations with the Canadians.

The social and economic roots of the Métis involvement in the resistance are to be found in the changing environment of the 1860s both in Red River and in the interior. On the eve of the resistance the Métis were living in an increasingly smaller and more difficult world, well aware of the English hatred and uncertain as to the future. Even their own society had become more polarized since the 1840s, with more and more goods accruing to the wealthy merchant farmers of the parishes of St. Boniface, St. Vital and St. Norbert—a wealth based on the local grain market and on the lucrative St. Paul freight contracts with the Company and other private merchants.[10] Many of these teamster princes had accommodated themselves to the Company and sat on its Councils, while retaining pride in their heritage and culture. The majority of the Métis however squatted along the Red and Assiniboine Rivers and while the women tended the poor barley and potato patches, the men pursued the last of the buffalo, traded independently, or plied the Company's freight boats. The proceeds of the diminishing hunt and the Company's meagre wages could also be supplemented by the fall fisheries.

The Métis were in competition for the declining resources both of the plain and the river lot. To those who had seized the opportunity offered by free trade overland carting in furs accrued an increasing proportion of Red River's wealth. An examination of livestock holdings serves as an example of this growing concentration. The average number of oxen per family increased for

Average No. of Calves per Family

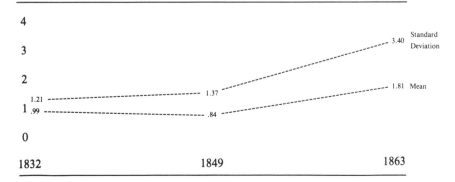

Average No. of Horses per Family

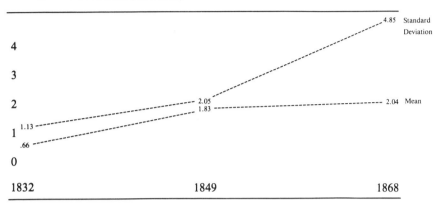

Average No. of Oxen per Family

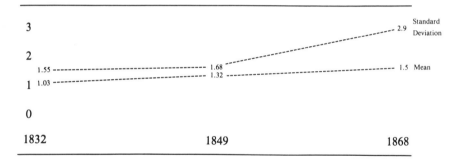

Average No. of Cows per Family

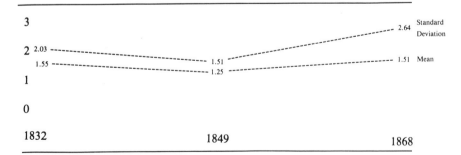

example from 1.3 in 1849 to 1.5 per family in 1868, the average number of cows per family from 1.3 to 1.5, the average number of calves per family from .8 to 1.8, and the average number of horses from 1.8 to 2.0 But a disproportionate share of this new wealth fell to the merchant farmer. While in 1849 he rarely had more than the average number of horses, by 1868 he had at least twice as many. The same is true for oxen and calves.[11]

Wealth was particularly concentrated in the parishes of St. Vital, St. Boniface and St. Norbert. These parishes produced more than half of Métis Red River's grain and potatoes and possessed most of the livestock. The situation in the other parishes was less buoyant. As late as 1867, for example, one-half of the Métis grew no grain. The majority of these were concentrated in the new parishes on the Red and Assiniboine where the plains hunters, the boatmen and some of the freighters had settled. This growing disparity between rich and poor was not evident in English-speaking Red River.[12]

The fragility of the Métis economy was particularly evident in 1868. In 1867 the Métis had harvested some 15,000 bushels of grain; in 1868 the locusts left only 1,200 bushels. The potato crop was equally devasted, the usual 12,000 crop was reduced to 5,000. Those of means managed to buy from the stored surpluses of English Red River, while the hardest hit—the landless, the squatters and the labourers—were only saved from starvation by the charity of the Executive Relief Committee of the Council of Assiniboia.[13]

Neither the merchant farmers not the landless labourers, would rejoice at the Canadian union. That connection would spell an end of the commercial and agricultural hegemony of the St. Boniface merchant farmer elite. P. G. Laurie, a Canadian reporter, viewed their predicament with concern. He sympathized with the Métis fear that the more energetic Canadians would destroy the freighters by introducing railroads and tariffs.[14] Many of the Métis were also afraid that their small, internal grain markets would quickly fall into the hands of the more efficient and "better connected" Canadian farmer. These economic concerns would have predisposed many to accept both Riel's arguments and actions.

Indeed some of the first to become involved in the resistance were affiliated with the merchant group. John Bruce, the first President of the Métis provisional government, was in the employ of two of the more prosperous Red River merchants. Riel for his part drew much of his support from amongst the Lagimodière side of his family that figured prominently amongst the merchant farmers. This is not to say that the class supported Riel with equal vigour.

Piere Delorme, one of the first to support Riel, was well aware that the coming of the Canadians would end Métis prosperity. He demanded the title to the land the Métis occupied, 200 additional acres for each of their children, and Indian status for their wives, which would allow the Métis to benefit from any Indian land settlement. Most important, he wanted the tract of land lying south of the Assiniboine reserved as a self-governing colony free from all taxation. There the Métis merchant would be protected by a free trade zone.[15] The zone was an impossibility but the Métis merchant group argued vehemently during the Red River conventions for exemption from customs duties. The best they were able to negotiate was a three year period of grace before the

Canadian duties would be applied.

If the merchant farmers provided vocal support for Riel during the resistance, the Métis boatmen provided the muscle. There is some evidence to indicate that it was these people who manned the Upper Fort and quashed the English counter-insurrections. The tradition of mutiny for the boatmen was an old one. In 1859 the Company had tried to redress the "unpopularity" of the Company's service by increasing wages and bettering the treatment of the boatmen.[16] Despite these efforts, the situation became so uncontrollable that the Company decided in the late 1860s to by-pass the brigade whenever conditions made steamboat or cart traffic viable. William Mactavish was prepared to start by replacing the Saskatchewan brigades.

> It would in the end enable us to do without the Portage boats, the crews of which have not become a perfect nuisance from their mutinous conduct and unwillingness to carry out any engagement.[17]

The causes of the mutinies were many. While the wages of the boatmen increased from £14 to £20 per trip in the early 1860s, they were still well below those offered for general labour either in Canada or the United States, something of which the men were well aware. Even in Red River itself more money was to be made in haying for the more prosperous farmers than freighting for the Bay Company. Secondly the conditions on the trip were far from tolerable. The boats were poorly repaired, they were often overloaded and they frequently broke apart. Equally important, by the early 1860s the free traders had ensconced themselves in the Norway House area. They quite enjoyed subverting the Company's brigades. In 1863 at Norway House they liquored up the Oxford House boatmen and persuaded them not only to desert the Company, but to trade the Company's furs.[18]

A more fundamental malaise amongst the Métis boatmen was the breakdown of the hierarchical, almost military society, that had been the backbone of the Company. It was a society in which the men and officers knew their place, and in which each recognized the others' rights and responsibilities. The Company's officers were responsible for the welfare and well being of their servants. Generally the men were responsible for providing the Company's labour. The best of this hierarchical society was seen at the Company's posts in the late eighteenth and early nineteenth century.[19] Disenchantment was certainly prevalent in the upper ranks as early as the 1830s because of the Company's reluctance to employ the officers' mixed-blood children at anything but menial tasks. The change in the Company's management in the 1860s, and the retirement of the old officers in the 1850s probably resulted in the breakdown of the compact between the servants and officers.[20]

During the winter of 1869-70 the boatmen, as was their habit, returned to Red River for the fall fisheries and a comfortable winter. When Riel needed men to seize the Upper Fort on November 19, 1869, in order to consolidate his hold on the settlement, the boatmen were ready to harass the Company they so hated. To them the seizure of the Upper Fort would be the greatest mutiny of all. In 1869 the Upper For Garry clerk indignantly recorded approximately one hundred and fifty individual Métis who were in receipt of cash and sundries that Riel had confiscated from the Company. Most were at the Upper Fort from its seizure in the winter of 1869 to the spring of 1870. In comparing these names with the 1868 Executive Relief Committee census, none, it would appear, were men of property or even settlers of modest affluence. They must have been either freighters or labourers.[21] It could also be assumed that the plains winterers were not manning the fort for they were not known to be in the settlement during the resistance of 1869-70. Although they threatened involvement they seem to have confined their activities to the interior.

If the men at the Upper Fort were indeed the boatmen, this would account for the difficulties in the Northern brigades in the summer following the insurrection. Norway House reported that during the winter of the resistance both men and Indians (were kept) in such a state of

> excitement that the trade was affected considerably. Still the winter and spring passed without trouble excepting two mutinies amongst our people which in both instances resulted in our favour.[22]

In the spring, when the boatmen arrived from Red River, the situation deteriorated even further. Of the twelve boat crews initially engaged in Red River for York Factory only four arrived, the others having refused to embark. Similarly, of the nine boat crews scheduled for Portage la Loche, only three would go beyond Norway House and even then there was no guarantee that they would proceed further than Grand Rapids.[23] The boatmen were so unmanageable that the Company resolved to abandon the boat brigades for overland transport forever. The "mutiny" at the settlement may have been broken by the Imperial armies, but it continued in the interior with no small degree of success.

While the greatest mutiny of the boat brigades can be said to have taken place in Red River, the uprising of the winterers was confined to the plains. The buffalo were disappearing quickly in the 1860s, the only sightings being in the South Saskatchewan and Cypress Hills country. Consequently, the shrunken hunting territories increased the potential for conflict between the Blackfeet and Cree, the Cree and the Métis, and the Métis and the whites.[24] William Mactavish was most fearful that all would eventually fight for the last buffalo in the Cypress Hills.[25] The Métis especially resented the Company's continuing demands for supplies. While they realized that the Company was their livelihood, they also knew that it would be their death. The whole of the plains was ripe for a particularly black and vicious storm.

Initially the winterers from the Saskatchewan River District as fars south as Minnesota had every intention of joining the fray at Red River. To them it was not so much a struggle to preserve a Métis lifestyle, as a protest against the Company tyranny. In 1869 Mactavish feared that unless the Riel business was settled soon "the Country (would) be overrun by a lawless horde of sympathizers from Minnesota and Dakotah who under the pretext of aiding would assume the direction of the movement."[26] Mactavish's fears materialized to the extent that the winterers did attempt to seize control of the Saskatchewan and Qu'Appelle districts. In the *New Nation* of March 4th, 1870 rumour had it, that in the Shoal and Swan River districts, the freemen had "leaped" to arms, and captured some of Fort Pelly's outposts. While this proved more fiction than fact, the outpost of White Horse Plains was captured and its cattle confiscated and slaughtered. Oak Point and Lake Manitobah posts were also attacked. At Oak Point Mr. Macdonald, the clerk in charge, barely escaped being taken prisoner. He was pursued by a number of Métis but managed to reach Manitobah Post safely. He barricaded himself there and along with eight Scottish servants defended its property against forty Métis. The situation was so threatening that the Chief Trader at Qu'Appelle bundled the furs and slipped them across the border in the dark of night.[27]

While those at Manitobah Post were convinced that their stand had saved the Swan River District from the ravages of the winterers, the credit is in fact due Pascal Breland, the son-in-law of Cuthbert Grant, one time warden of the plains. He spent much of the winter of 1869-70 in the Qu'Appelle, Saskachewan country exhorting the Métis to peace. Breland had, for some still unknown reason, a personal dislike for Louis Riel, and perhaps because of his connection with Grant, still had a fondness for the Company. Had he not acted, the Riel protest might have spread like the proverbial prairie fire and consumed the whole of the Saskatchewan country in conflagration.[28]

While knowledge of Red River's social, economic and constitutional history is crucial to understanding the unfolding of events in 1869, so is an understanding of religion. The Métis of Red River were devoutly Catholic, but it must be emphasized that they were not slaves to the institutional church. They might listen to their clergy, but they were quite capable of making individual decisions. The influence of religion amongst the boatmen and plainsmen in fact, depended more upon the character of the individual priests like Father Richot of St. Norbert. There is no real evidence that he determined the course of events during 1869, although he certainly preached resistance from the Sunday pulpit. But his scheme for a Catholic theocracy on the Red, governed by the Catholic clergy, was certainly not seized upon by either the merchant farmers or the boatmen. He was listened to because he struck a responsive chord—Métis culture and religion was in danger from the coming Protestant ascendancy.

The Métis were willing to listen to the warnings of the clergy because of their experiences in the early 1860s. In the first years of that decade the Rev. G.O. Corbett had launched a vicious anti-Catholic campaign in the settlement's newspaper. He not only pointed out to all who would listen, the threat of a popish plot to gain supremacy in Red River, but the innate inferiority of Catholic religion, Catholic education, Catholic medicine and Catholics in general. So virulent did sentiments become between the Protestant and Catholic mixed-bloods that James Ross, rather moderate in his anti-Catholicism and at times a restraining influence, refused to publish an obituary of Sister Valade, one of the most venerated of the Saint-Boniface sisters. Ross also became the object of a death threat from Louis Riel, père, if he continued the anti-Catholic editorials of the *Nor'Wester*.[29]

Thus when Ritchot and the priests at the forks preached the unfortunate consequences of a Protestant supremacy in 1869, the Métis could only believe. They worked because Protestantism implied bigotry and the probable suppression of their cultural institutions. The merchant farmers feared that, because of their religion, they would be excluded from the commercial elite of the future. Similarly the English mixed-bloods began to believe that every action by a Catholic clergyman was the result of a string pulled by the Pope. So, during the events of 1869, all believed to some degree the warning of their respective clergy. The events of 1869-70 may not have been a sectarian conflict, but the flavouring was strong.

This brief examination of the social, economic, and religious background does not pretend to suggest a new interpretation of the Riel resistance, rather it attempts to suggest perspectives from which new insights can be gleaned with further research. For example, was the resistance really anything more than a grand mutiny of the boat brigades? Was it an expression of the fears of an old Catholic merchant farmer elite of displacement, isolation in a new, unsought Protestant dominated order? Was the resistance nothing more than a hysterical reaction by the Métis to the religious railings of the Canadians and their English half-breed supporters? Ultimately this paper suggests that less energy should be spent on analyzing the resistance itself and more on discovering its roots. The resistance has many secret faces. Most of these have yet to be uncovered by the historian.

5

The Métis:
The People and
the Term

John Foster

Abstract

The confusion surrounding the meaning of the term Métis, people of mixed Indian and Euro-Canadian ancestry, arises from an inadequate historical understanding. The buffalo hunting Métis on the plains provide few problems of identification. But others such as the "Iroquois" in Alberta and the "English Halfbreeds" are difficult to categorize. An historical understanding emphasizing two trading systems, the St. Lawrence Great Lakes trading system and the Hudson Bay trading system, each with its particular fur trade tradition, offers a solution. The Métis, through particular historical circumstances, arose out of the "broker-trader" role in the St. Lawrence tradition. In the Bay tradition this role was an "Indian" role. The people of mixed ancestry in the Bay tradition, who did not become Métis, arose from the Home Guard Cree, the post provisioners. In identifying people of mixed ancestry historically, one must take into account their own view of themselves.

Resume

La confusion qui règne autour de la signification du terme Métis, population issue d'un mélange entre Indiens et Euro-Canadiens, vient d'une perception éronée de l'histoire. Les Métis des plaines, qui chassent le bison, posent peu de problèmes d'identification. Il est plus difficile par contre, de savoir à quelle catégorie appartiennent les "Iroquois" de l'Alberta, et les "English Halfbreeds." On peut trouver une solution à travers une approche de l'histoire qui ferait ressortir deux systèmes de commerces, celui du St. Laurent et des Grands Lacs d'une part, et d'autre part celui de la Baie d'Hudson, l'un et l'autre avec sa propre tradition dans le commerce de la fourrure. C'est du rôle de "marchands-courtiers" propre à la tradition du St.-Laurent, que sont issus les Métis, par le biais de circonstances historiques particulières. Dans la tradition de la Baie, ce rôle était le rôle de l'"Indien". Les populations issues d'un mélange de races, dans la tradition de la Baie, qui ne sont pas devenues des Métis, provenaient, elles, du mélange avec les Home Guard Cree, leurs futurs fournisseurs. Il faut, pour identifier d'un point de vue historique des populations issues d'un mélange de races, considérer d'abord l'idée que ces peuples se font d'eux-mêmes.

IN THE CANADIAN West much confusion surrounds the use of the term "Métis". While scholars and laymen alike agree that the term refers to persons of mixed Indian and Euro-Canadian ancestry, it is difficult to obtain a more precise definition. "Métis" can refer to individuals and communities who derive some of ther cultural practices from non-Indian native communities whose origins lie in the pre-1870 West. In other instances, the term is used to refer to individuals whose circumstances of birth suggest "Métis" as preferable to the frequently pejorative term, "Halfbreed". On occasion, the term also encompasses non-status Indians. Thus, in one circumstance, the term conveys a sense of cultural identity and, in another, a quasi-legal status. Perhaps the most useful view of the term today is as a label identifying a segment of western society which, in addition to recognizing an ancestry of mixed Indian and Euro-Canadian origins, seeks to realize various interests through particular political goals and actions. It is possible that such Métis cultural cohesiveness is not now evident.[1] Even without such a development, significant questions emerge as to the cultural links between the nineteenth century Métis and those to whom the term refers today. In essence such questions are problems in historical understanding.

Confusion in the use of the term "Métis" is not new; it existed prior to 1870. There would appear to be agreement on what might be termed the classical image of the Métis as conveyed in some of Paul Kane's paintings[2] and Alexander Ross's writings.[3] The French-speaking, Roman Catholic, non-Indian native, buffalo hunters of the Red River Settlement emerged distinct from the sociocultural mosaic of the period and the region. As these people constituted Louis Riel's following (a principal reason for Canadian interest in their history), there seems to be some justification for labelling them as a distinct entity. Yet, problems in terminology emerge after a short perusal of the literature. What of the other non-Indian native peoples of the pre-1870 West who did not fit the "classical" image of the Métis? After the 1840's, what of the English-speaking, Protestant, buffalo hunters of Portage la Prairie, Prince Albert and Fort Victoria east of Fort Edmonton?[4] Did not their mixed Indian and Euro-Canadian ancestry as well as their way of life qualify them as Métis in spite of their predilection for the English tongue and Protestant Churchmen? And what of others? The French and Saulteaux speaking Roman Catholic, voyageur-farmers in Red River and their neighbours, the English-speaking, Protestant, farmer-tripmen and occasional merchants—could they be considered "Métis"?[5] The French and Cree-speaking, Roman Catholic, buffalo hunters of the North Saskatchewan river valley would appear to fit the "classical" image of the Métis with ease.[6] But, what of their neighbours to the north in the valleys of the Peace and Athabasca Rivers, the Cree-speaking, Roman Catholic, "Iroquois" trapper-hunters?[7] Many of their descendants would demand halfbreed scrip rather than treaty status at the Treaty Eight signings in 1899.[8] Were these people Indians, Métis or . . .? In attempting to answer these questions writers have chosen a variety of terms to describe people of mixed ancestry who were not considered to be Indians.

Most writers dealing with the pre-1870 West accept the existence of two recognizable entities of mixed ancestry. The Métis, occasionally styled the *Bois Brulés* or *Chicot,*[9] provoke little debate although it is not always clear to whom the term applies. It is the "British" and "Protestant" segment as opposed to the "French" and "Catholic" part of the mixed-blood population which appears to provide most of the difficulties. The term "Halfbreed" is used in a similar way to the term "Métis", capitalized and uncapitalized.[10] But, it is apparent the term can apply to both collectivities as well. Scots Halfbreeds, English Métis and *Métis écossais* are other favourites. More recent additions have included "Country-born" and "Rupert'slander".[11] The confusion surrounding some of the terms suggests that some writers have an inadequate understanding of the times and regions in which some of the terms flourished and to whom they applied.

Reflecting their own cultural antecedents and the traditions of interpretation in their discipline, historians studying the pre-1870 West have tended to emphasize a metropolitan perspective in viewing the passage of events. Whether it is Paris or London, Montreal or, near the end of the period, Toronto, the extension of metropolitan influence and control for purposes of resource exploitation is viewed empathetically.[12] The interests of the populations of these centres and more frequently the interests of their agents in the hinterland are central to the historian's narrative. The primary sources themselves heighten the sense of the predominance of metropolitan interests because these documents were the creations of the agents or metropolitan centres. While amenable to analysis from a hinterland perspective most of the documents lend themselves more readily to an analysis of processes central to metropolitan concerns. The value of this approach is evident in the sophisticated and sensitive analysis of the actions of men and institutions whose cultural ties lay with the distant homeland.[13] Too frequently these same subjects can suffer from superficial analysis and dehumanizing assessment in other disciplinary approaches. Yet in historical analysis the narrative too often shifts its focus when the interests of the metropolis no longer hold sway. To obtain an acceptable historical understanding of the pre-1870 West, historians must attempt to perceive hinterland happenings in terms of a hinterland perspective as well as the traditional metropolitan perspective. One without the other is inadequate.

A basic premise in elaborating a hinterland perspective for the pre-1870 West is that the importance of the fur trade lay as much in the changing ways of life of the participants as it did in the commercial and political processes by which the metropolis extended and elaborated its interests in the hinterland. From a hinterland perspective, the appearance of agents from the different metropolitan centres introduced not only new material goods but new social elements into Western society. In adapting their ways to new realities the newcomers and their goods stimulated Indian responses whose particular nature was determined by their cultural antecedents and fur trade roles such as Home Guard-provisioners, middleman-traders and trappers.[14] Over time, the particular nature of influences emanating from specific metropolitan centres left distinctive cultural legacies. As these legacies were incorporated in the various ways of life of the participants in each of the two trading systems, they created two distinct fur trade traditions.

For French mercantilists in the early modern period, commerce was a key means of enhancing the interests of the French state.[15] Thus, the Government of Louis XIV saw the fur trading system of the St. Lawrence-Great Lakes region as a tool of imperial expansion rather than a reason for it. Fur trade alliances with Indian bands were the means of extending French influence into the interior of the North American continent and denying its resources to European rivals. Diplomacy and the military as much as the market-place furnished the skills necessary for survival in the St. Lawrence trading system.[16] After the Conquest, the British, as evidenced in Pontiac's uprising in 1763, abandoned French practices at their peril. The emergence of a hostile United States of America to the south of the Great Lakes in the closing decades of the eighteenth century emphasized, in the mind of British colonial authorities, the necessity of adopting the French practice of establishing politico-military alliances with Indian bands.[17] Such alliances depended upon the exchange of furs for European goods. The success of French practice, which rested as much on the social ties of kinship as it did on political and economic interest,[18] led the Highland Scots, who succeeded to the control of the St. Lawrence fur trade system at Montreal, to think more in terms of elaboration rather than replacement when adapting their traditions to the legacy of *Canadien* ways.[19] In this trading system, of course, both the Indian and the Euro-Canadian faced the continuing challenge of adapting traditions to changing realities. The coherence of the process evolved what can be termed a St. Lawrence fur trade tradition. Central to this tradition and of crucial importance to both Indians and Euro-Canadians was the "Indian trader."

With the destruction of Huronia at the hands of the Iroquois in 1649-50, the French on the St. Lawrence had to exercise increasing control over the conduct of the fur trade if their alliance system was to survive. To this end the *coureur de bois* emerged.[20] Reflecting the military, diplomatic and merchant-adventuring skills of their heritage they established, through marriages and adoptions, the necessary bonds of kinship with Indian bands. Political and commercial activity depended upon such social ties. In time, with specialization and sophistication, the *coureur de bois* gave way to the voyageur on one hand and the commandant-trader on the other.[21] Critical to the French tradition was the practice of carrying trade goods to the Indian trappers and returning with furs.[22] Expeditions from major forts established outposts and from them parties visited bands in their hunting and trapping grounds. Frequently ties of kinship linked the commandants of major forts, the bourgeois heading the outpost, and the trader who led the *en dérouine* party.[23] For both Euro-Canadians and Indians this latter figure, a kinsman playing a mediational or broker role, was crucial to maintaining the fur trade alliance. In time, most of these brokers were of mixed Indian and Euro-Canadian ancestry.

Jacqueline Peterson, in a timely article, describes a most interesting family survival strategy resting upon "middleman" control of trading activity in the Great Lakes region.[24] A newly arrived trader would undertake a short term "country marriage" with a woman of a prominent family in an Indian band to establish the kinship basis necessary for trading activity. Afterwards, possibly after other country marriages, a more permanent marriage with a *Canadien* woman of mixed Indian and *Canadien* ancestry or simply *Canadien* ancestry would be established. This wife would raise not only her own children but frequently the children of her husband by his "country wives." Later, some sons would follow in their father's footsteps and contract alliances with Indian women before undertaking more permanent marriages. Their sisters as well fulfilled a similar role, marrying potential competitors to facilitate "understandings". Several families appear to have survived the disruption of the Conquest by forming marriage alliances with incoming British traders.[25] These traders in turn quickly came to appreciate the advantage that such family ties conveyed in the hectic competition of the fur trade. The broker skills of a brother-in-law of mixed ancestry, leading an *en dérouine* party, were as crucial as British manufactures in achieving a successful trade.

With the founding of the Hudson's Bay Company in 1670, a second fur trading system came into existence. The Company's first half century dictated a strategy termed the "coast-side factory system."[26] This policy was criticized as the "sleep by the frozen sea."[27] The Company did not abandon on this policy and move into the interior in strength until the latter quarter of the eigh-

teenth century. As a result, trade with the Indians of the interior was controll-
ed by the Cree and Assiniboine middlemen.[28] These trading chiefs filled the
broker role for the interior Indians in the Hudson Bay trading system. For the
Home Guard Cree bands living in the environs of the coastal factories,
however, the goodwill of the post commander was crucial to their interests.[29]
He was styled "Unkimow" or "patriarch," a position of pre-eminence in their
world. In the trading post among the British-born he occupied the highest
social position, received the greatest material benefits and exercised the most
power. To the Home Guard Cree, British-born servants and officers in the
trading post, he was the "Indian Trader" in the Hudson Bay tradition.

In each of the fur trade traditions the inhabitants made the basic socio-
cultural distinction between Indians and Europeans. The distinction was not
one of race; rather, it emphasized ways of life. This is most apparent in the
manner in which the inhabitants classified children of mixed European and Indian ancestry.[30] In both fur trade traditions the child was associated with the
mother and classified socio-culturally with her way of life. If the mother remained with the Indian band the child was an "Indian." In the Hudson Bay
tradition the term "Native" could be used as well, referring, it would appear,
to an "Indian" who had a real or fictive kinship tie with personnel in the
trading post. If the mother and child resided in the trading post for an extended period the child was "*Canadien*" or "*Scots*" (Euro-Canadian) in the St.
Lawrence traditions, and "English" in the posts of the Hudson's Bay Company.[31]

A circumstance recorded in York Factory Journals and Account Books in
the early 1760's demonstrates how the historical actors viewed themselves and
their fellows in the Bay traditions. Two Native youths, Robert and Thomas Inksetter, sons of tailor Robert Inksetter who served at the Bottom of the Bay
and York Factory from the early 1720's through to the late 1740's, enlisted as
servants in the Company's service on five year contracts.[32] In the parlance of
the Fort and the surrounding bands they had become English. After two years,
the young men requested permission to have wives live with them in the fort.[33]
Their request was refused on the grounds that, among the English, only the
commanding officer enjoyed this privilege.[34] With their Indian heritage allowing them an additional option to those enjoyed by British-born servants, the
brothers broke their contracts and left the Fort.[35] They undoubtedly lived with
bands who continued to trade with the Company and were known by name but
their English names did not survive their departure. As far as the Company's
records are concerned, Thomas and Robert Inksetter did not exist after 1761.[36]
They had ceased being "English" and had become "Indian" or "Native"
again.

It was in the St. Lawrence fur trade that a term first emerged distinguishing
a socio-cultural entity of mixed-Indian and Euro-Canadian ancestry from
either the Indian or Euro-Canadian in the West. By the second decade of the

nineteenth century the term "Métis" or the English equivalent "Halfbreed" identified the newly emerged collectivity.[37] It would appear that neither term, at least initially, was meant to be complimentary. "Halfbreed" apparently could suggest a child of a morganatic liaison or marriage while "Métis" could suggest "mongrel" rather than "mixed" as is frequently suggested.[38] Such terminology, however, did not necessarily indicate low social stutus for those to whom it applied. Rather, it seems plausible to suggest that such terms initially reflected the resentment of Euro-Canadians who found themselves dependent upon such individuals or more likely unable to effect marriage alliances which would tie such individuals to their interests. It would appear that the derogatory term was soon flaunted in the faces of those who used it by those to whom it referred. "Métis" was the term by which some families of mixed ancestry in the St. Lawrence tradition came to identify themselves.

In the region of the Red and Assiniboine River valleys in the first two decades of the nineteenth century, a second element, probably related to the first, became associated with the term "Métis." These were the provisioning bands of mixed ancestry who hunted buffalo in the region and through "recognized hunters"[39] supplied pemmican and dried meat to the traders. After 1810, as the North West Company entered the closing decade of fur trade competition challenged by a revitalized and modernizing Hudson's Bay Company, a kinship of traders to Indian bands or recognized hunters on the plains was critical to any hope of success. It was natural that North West Company officers would encourage these people, the "Métis", to see themselves as the "New Nation" whose interests were threatened by the arrival of the Selkirk settlers and the policies of the Hudson's Bay Company.[40] The events of the decade, focussing on the Battle of Seven Oaks, June 16, 1815, did not bring success to the North West Company but they caused the Métis to emerge as a self-conscious entity with a sense of a particular past and a particular destiny.

In the decade following the end of the fur trade competition in 1820, numerous families of mixed Indian and Euro-Canadian ancestry in the St. Lawrence tradition journeyed to Red River to join the Métis. As a result, differences amongst the Métis appeared. The pre-eminent elements were the plains hunters and the old training families. Others functioned as fishermen on the lakes to the north. Still others enlisted as voyageurs on the York boats of the Hudson's Bay Company and on private freighters.[41] In later years some Métis families, including the Riels, took concerted action to emphasize their French and Roman Catholic orientation in contrast to the life-styles of their neighbours.[42] As all these elements considered themselves "Métis" in Red River and were considered to be a single collectivity by other communities, the term would appear to be applicable beyond the limits of the Settlement.

The non-Indian native peoples in the St. Lawrence fur trade tradition, hunting buffalo from settlements near the North Saskatchewan river valley, apparently created few problems in being described as Métis. Throughout the half century before Confederation, individuals and families migrated from the region to Red River and a movement of individuals and families flowed in the opposite direction as well.[43] To the north in the valleys of the Peace and Athabasca rivers another distinctive people emerged in the St. Lawrence fur trade tradition. But were they Métis? A number certainly identified themselves as such and do so today.

In the late 1790's, finding the Indians of the Upper Saskatchewan and neighbouring river valleys harvesting furs according to their needs and not the needs of the traders, the North West Company brought into the interior as many as 200 Iroquois, Ottawa, Nipissing and Saulteaux trapper-voyageurs.[44] These eastern Indians, amongst whom the Iroquois predominated, had lifestyles that demanded more Euro-Canadian goods than did the Indians resident in the region. Accorded privileges of price, goods and social prestige similar to the trading families in the Great Lakes and Red River regions, the Iroquois radiated outward from Fort Edmonton. South of the Saskatchewan River many died in conflicts with members of the Blackfoot Confederacy. Others soon returned to the East. The remainder, joined by a few *Canadien* freemen flourished to the north and west. In spite of the tension between them and the Cree and Beaver peoples, the Iroquois were outstandingly successful. Taking wives from amongst the Cree they established the kinship ties that made them effective traders as well as hunters and trappers. The special relationship which they had enjoyed with the North West Company was continued with the Hudson's Bay Company after 1820 although in a somewhat attenuated form.[45] At the end of the century a number of descendants of these families chose scrip rather than treaty as, in their minds, they were not Indians, but Halfbreeds[46] or Métis who derived many of their ways from the St. Lawrence fur trading tradition.

In the Hudson Bay tradition in the early years of the nineteenth century, a term distinguishing a third community, distinct from the "Indians" or "Natives" and the "English" did not arise. In contrast to the St. Lawrence tradition in which the term "Métis" and its English equivalent "Halfbreed" arose, people in the Bay tradition remained "Native" or "English". It is noteworthy that Peter Fidler, a Hudson's Bay Company officer, and one of the first individuals to use the term "Halfbreed" in referring to peoples in the St. Lawrence tradition, did not apply the term to individuals in the Hudson Bay tradition.[47] Fidler's own children were clearly "English", not "Native" and certainly not "Halfbreeds". After 1820 a number of Hudson Bay "English" (the *Anglais* of the Métis) moved to Red River to become river lot farmers, tripmen in the York boats and private merchants.[48] They were joined by Hudson Bay Native kinsmen who in some instances joined them as "English". Others were encouraged to join Peguis's band of Saulteaux at the Indian village below the Red River Settlement.[49] The appearance of officers with British wives in the 1830's created problems of terminology for the Hudson Bay "English".[50] By the end of the 1840's they no longer saw themselves as English as evidenced in the strikingly belligerent manner in which a Hudson Bay English Anglican catechist referred to himself as "only Half-an-Englishman".[51] At the same time the term "Halfbreed" was taking on a definition separate from that of the Métis.

The Anglican missionaries who were involved with the Hudson Bay English used three terms to identify them. The term "half-caste" disappeared after Rev. John West's departure.[52] "Country-born", to distinguish them from the "Native-born", appeared as early as 1852.[53] However, "Halfbreed" was the most frequently encountered term in missionary writings.[54] This development was unfortunate as the term at the time was taking on racial and cultural connotations of a negative nature. The Hudson Bay English in Red River seem to have been as confused as their observers. Occasional references to "my Countrymen" demonstrate a sense of their distinctiveness from Indians and Métis.[55] When acting in concert with the Métis they used the term "Halfbreed" to refer to their collective interest.[56] Yet as mentioned previously this choice may have indeed been rather unfortunate.

Governor George Simpson of the Hudson's Bay Company's North American operations initially followed the Hudson Bay tradition in the use of the term "Native" to designate individuals of mixed ancestry.[57] Quite quickly he switched to the use of "Halfbreed", the term originating in the St. Lawrence tradition.[58] It is readily apparent that Simpson associated the term with individuals of mixed ancestry whose habits of life were at odds with his enthusiasm for "modernism" with its emphasis of efficiency of process whether comercial or administrative. Simpson could recall Hudson Bay English families such as the Cooks and the Birds whose concerns with privileges derived from rank and kinship emphasized the particularism that was the principal barrier to efficient process in the fur trade in Rupert's Land.[59] The Hudson Bay "English" in his experience were the unprogressive opponents of modernism. To Simpson it was obvious that their unsteady habits were functions of their "Indian" ancestry. His "character" book demonstrates clearly that he was biased against individuals of mixed ancestry.[60] Nevertheless, Simpson was too able a modernist to allow his prejudice to interfere with his recognition of demonstrated merit. The career of Chief Factor William Sinclair, Junior, the descendant of an old Hudson Bay English family, is a case in point. It would appear that Simpson simply removed the individual from the category of his prejudice while still retaining his prejudice against "Halfbreeds". To Simpson, Chief Factor William Sinclair, Junior, was an effective officer, not a "Halfbreed."[61] Officers recently arrived from Great Britain shared Simpson's views on "Halfbreeds"[62] whose traditionalist ways were seen as antagonistic to the effective and efficient operation of the fur trade. By mid-century it would appear that the term "Halfbreed" had come to encompass all persons of mixed ancestry from both fur trade traditions. Unfortunately, the concept was essentially negative.

The Hudson Bay English apparently never did successfully resolve their problem of creating a term round which they could identify their common interests. They saw themselves as distinct from the Métis.[63] Others viewed them as a socio-cultural element distinct from Métis. In these circumstances, scholars have faced a labelling problem. While a plethora of terms has been used to identify them for purposes of study, no single term has gained wide acceptance. Perhaps in spite of its serious limitations "Red River Halfbreed" may yet emerge as the most useful term to identify this cultural entity.

The same problem does not emerge with the term "Métis". With a conceptual framework that equates a hinterland perspective with a metropolitan perspective, two distinct trading systems, each with its particular tradition, can be seen to emerge. In each tradition the person of mixed ancestry was socio-culturally identified with his way of life, not his biological heritage. Particular historical circumstances saw some individuals, who tended to be of mixed ancestry, emerge as distinct entities. In the Hudson Bay tradition these individuals emerged from Home Guard bands, not the middleman trading bands. In the St. Lawrence tradition historical circumstances singled out the traders and the provisioning hunters for recognition and exaltation. The events of the decade before the signing of the Deed Poll in 1821 provided the basis for the folk history of the "New Nation". Beyond the limits of the Red and Assiniboine river valleys, the term identified socio-cultural elements derived from the St. Lawrence tradition who functioned as trader-brokers and as provisioners. Thus the hunters of mixed ancestry in the North Saskatchewan river valley, many of whom were more familiar with Cree than French, were Métis as well. Similarly, the "Iroquois" of North Western Alberta were considered Métis people. It was the trader-broker role and the provisioning role in the St. Lawrence tradition that called forth the existence of the Métis. These same roles would determine the nature of their culture. Elements of that culture survive among some Métis people today.

6

Louis Schmidt: A Forgotten Métis

Raymond Huel

ON NOVEMBER 6, 1924, a 91 year old Métis passed away in St. Louis, a small village 25 miles south of Prince Albert. The death of Louis Schmidt passed unnoticed outside his family and acquaintances. *Le Patriote de L'Ouest*, a French language weekly published in Prince Albert, referred to the deceased as a great Christian and patriot whose life recalled the momentous transformations that had taken place in the West in the last seventy years.[1] Twenty-four years earlier, *Le Patriote* had published Schmidt's memoirs but these lines in an obscure journal had not made their author widely known.[2]

Louis Schmidt was born on December 4, 1844, at Old Fort on Lake Athabasca. His father was a fisherman employed by the Hudson's Bay Company and his mother was the daughter of a Red River guide. The origin of the family name is obscure. In his memoirs, Schmidt states that his paternal grandfather was Nicholas Andrews an employee of the Hudson's Bay Company who had taken a Métis woman as a wife. Andrews allegedly abandoned her and his three year old son and returned to England in 1824. The wife later married Pierre Laferté and Schmidt claimed that his father was always known by the name Laferté.[3] Schmidt's birth certificate, on the other hand, records his baptismal name as Louis Smith and his father's as Alfred Smith.[4] According to Schmidt's memoirs, the name Schmidt was given to him by Bishop Taché of St. Boniface because the clergyman believed that it was his real name.[5] It may very well be that the name Smith was too Protestant and English whereas the name Schmidt would be more acceptable in French Catholic circles.

In 1854, Schmidt arrived in St. Boniface where he received his early education. Four years later, in 1858, Schmidt, along with two other Métis children, Louis Riel and Daniel McDougall, was selected by Taché to further their education in colleges in Quebec. Schmidt attended the College de St. Hyacinthe and left in 1861 during his third year of study. Schmidt cited ill health and the damp climate as reasons for his premature departure but there is evidence to suggest that there were other factors. Upon his return to Red River, the young Métis asked Bishop Taché to forgive him for the sorrow that his misfortune and conduct had caused.[6] A few months later, Schmidt, referring to himself as an "unworthy protégé" wrote to say that he owed Taché a greater debt than he could ever repay and promised to mend his ways.[7] The nature of these transgressions is unknown but it is obvious that Schmidt found solace in prayer and religion and his gratitude vis-à-vis Taché in particular and the clergy in general grew over the years. These orthodox convictions and attachment to the clergy would have a profound influence on his interpretation of Louis Riel's role and motive in the Rebellion of 1885.

In St. Boniface, Schmidt made copies of Father Lacombe's Cree dictionary and grammar for other missionaries and assisted the clergy in neighboring parishes. In 1863, he accompanied Father André in his peace mission among the American Sioux. Afterwards, he worked for an American company that had a contract to deliver mail between Abercombie, Devil's Lake and Helena.

Upon returning to St. Boniface in May, 1868, the most striking change Schmidt noticed was that the population was becoming politicized, even the Métis. When Riel returned in July, Schmidt visited him and stayed with him for some time. They discussed the changes that were taking place and resolved to become involved in public issues when the opportunity presented itself.[8] In the meantime, Schmidt joined the caravans freighting goods between the United States and Red River. When he returned from one of these voyages on November 8, 1869, he found Fort Garry occupied by Riel and the Métis. He marked that the Métis were quiet and orderly and that they had begun this serious enterprise in prayer and meditation. After taking care of his affairs, Schmidt went to the Fort to stay with Riel and became his secretary in the "first" provisional government.[9] In February, 1870, Schmidt became assistant secretary of state in the reorganized provisional government. He prudently left Red River when Wolseley's expedition arrived but returned a short time later and was not harrassed.

Schmidt was elected to the first Legislative Assembly of Manitoba as the representative for St. Boniface West. He lost the election of 1874 but four years later he succeeded in defeating Maxime Lépine in St. Francois-Xavier East by the narrow margin of four votes. When the third legislature was dissolved in November, 1878, Schmidt did not seek re-election.

A short while later, Schmidt decided to follow in the footsteps of his confrères and immigrate to the North-West Territories. With funds provided by Taché, he was able to purchase oxen, carts and the necessary supplies and equipment. After examining land in the Duck Lake area, Schmidt resolved to settle on the south branch of the Saskatchewan River some six miles north of St. Laurent de Grandin. By September, 1880, eight half breed families had already established themselves in the area and Schmidt informed Taché that more were coming because the land was of excellent quality and there was lots of wood.[10]

The arrival of a large number of Manitoba Métis accentuated problems associated with the homestead legislation. There were difficulties in obtaining bona fide homesteads; there were complications arising from scrip claims and demands for river lots. In 1880, Schmidt, at the request of the local Métis, wrote the federal authorities informing them of existing grievances. In the summer of 1882, a large meeting was held in St. Laurent to voice dissatisfaction with the *status quo* and Schmidt acted as secretary. At about the same time, the Métis led by Charles Nolin, petitioned Ottawa to have Schmidt appointed assistant agent at the Dominion Lands Office in Prince Albert. He did not obtain the position despite the intercession of Joseph Royal, M.P. for Provencher, on his behalf.[11]

In January, 1884, Schmidt left his farm and took up residence in Prince Albert where he found employment as a clerk in a lawyer's office. A few weeks later he wrote to Taché asking him to use his influence to obtain the position in the Lands Office. Schmidt claimed that his appointment would help the Métis who had few supporters in administrative circles. He stated that he did not enjoy his present employment and that it might be terminated at any moment due to the difficult times. Furthermore, his employer treated him impertinently.[12]

While moving to Prince Albert, Schmidt met Baptiste Arcand, one of Gabriel Dumont's close associates, who was on his way to a meeting of French and English half-breeds. During their conversation Schmidt suggested that Riel should be asked to help the Métis obtain redress for their grievances. Schmidt was present at the May 6, 1884, meeting at Lindsay School where it was decided to issue an invitation to Riel. He was asked to be part of the delegation which would go to Montana to confer with Riel and he accepted. In the meantime, he received the coveted position in the Lands Office and advised the others that he could not accompany them. Later, when Riel arrived in the District of Saskatchewan, Schmidt obtained permission from his superior to visit him at Charles Nolin's house in St. Laurent. Schmidt offered his services to Riel who advised him to remain at the Lands Office where he could do more good for the Métis cause.[13]

In July, 1884, Riel addressed a public meeting at Treston Hall in Prince Albert. Schmidt remarked that, while Riel spoke at length, his declarations were vague and his speech lacked the vitality of earlier ones. While in Prince Albert, Riel stayed with Schmidt and together they visited their mutual friend, Father André, with whom they had lengthy discussions.[14]

Schmidt's role in the events of 1884-85 never has been fully explored. In his biography of Gabriel Dumont, George Woodcock claims that Schmidt was a man of indecisive character, an individual who feared the loss of his government appointment and, hence remained "on the verge of events throughout the coming period of agitation and rebellion".[15] Schmidt was not unaware or unmoved by the problems of the Métis. He had made numerous representations to the Department of Interior on their behalf and, as an employee of the Lands Office, he rendered them invaluable services. As a married man with a family and debts there is no doubt that he was concerned with safeguarding his employment.

He had good reason to be uneasy because there were some within the anti-French element who envied his position and who were trying to discredit him in the eyes of the administration by implicating him in the agitation taking place. Consequently, Schmidt began keeping a series of detailed notes on developments among the Métis in St. Laurent between July, 1884, and April, 1885. This 61 page document was sent to Bishop Taché who was to use its contents to defend Schmidt should the need arise.[16]

In addition, Schmidt was regarded with suspicion by some of the English-speaking residents of Prince Albert. To forestall innuendoes that he was a spy for the rebels some of his close friends (Father André, Thomas McKay and George Duck) urged him to join the local militia which had been formed to protect the town against an attack. Schmidt presented himself before Colonel Sproat and joined shortly before the hostilities began. During the night of March 26-27, he was wakened and ordered to join his company at the barracks without any explanation. On his way to the barracks he decided to stop at Father André's house in order to make his confession and to obtain details as to what was going on. Schmidt was stopped by a patrol and brought back under guard. Despite his explanations, he was not released until late next morning and only after Father André had spoken to the commander.[17]

Another reason why Schmidt kept these detailed notes was that he had a premonition the agitation would get out of hand and he wanted to make an accurate record of what transpired. Shortly after Riel's arrival in July, 1884, Schmidt wrote that the "movement" was above all an attempt to unite the people and make all their grievances known to the authorities by means of a memorial. He remarked that Riel's presence generated concern among moderate individuals and enthusiasm among the revolutionary minded. The Métis, infuriated by the government's indifference, regarded Riel as a powerful man who could obtain satisfaction from Ottawa. For his part, Riel moderated passions and spoke only of peaceful means. Despite these affirmations, there were some who felt that Riel had not revealed all his plans. Schmidt noted that Riel had made a good impression on Father André who was more favourable than hostile to his proposals. Nevertheless, the clergyman feared that some hidden machination might push the movement toward different objectives.[18]

In August, 1884, Schmidt wrote that Riel was becoming infuriated with the defiant attitude of the clergy. On August 17, Schmidt described a heated conversation between himself, Riel, Maxime Lépine and Father André in which Riel openly proposed heretical and revolutionary ideas. Riel also declared that he no longer had complete confidence in the clergy even in doctrinal matters. Riel went on to inform Father André that he had a special and divine mission to fulfill.[19]

An astute observer, Schmidt was not unaware that a significant number of prominent, influential individuals in Prince Albert had encouraged and supported Riel from time to time. According to Schmidt, this emboldened Riel who often told Father André that he had the support of hundreds of men in Prince Albert. Schmidt also expressed his concern over the detrimental effects of Riel's presence on the Indian tribes in the Duck Lake area. According to Schmidt, some of the Indians were demanding nothing less than a new treaty with the government.[20]

By December, 1884, Schmidt had nothing but contempt for Riel's agitation. He claimed that Riel was no longer concerned with redressing legitimate grievances of the Métis but with having the government negotiate with him as a sovereign power to establish a new constitution and government in the North-West. Schmidt believed that the true purpose of the movement was to obtain lucrative posts for the principal instigators—Riel, Lépine and Nolin.[21] According to Schmidt, Riel's absurd theories appealed to demagogues and the Métis who, in their blind faith, could not distinguish right from wrong. Riel no longer felt bound by any restraints and Schmidt believed that Father André was the only one who could prevent him from implementing his plans. Schmidt was convinced that even Taché could do nothing to make Riel act in a reasonable manner because it was especially against the bishop that Riel held a grudge.[22]

Schmidt viewed Riel's religious heresies with even more repugnance. At first, Schmidt did not associate Riel's heretical ideas with a pronounced determination to execute them but with a lack of serious reflection or a means of making a point in a heated argument. Afterwards Schmidt felt that Riel would abandon his sham religious practices when they were no longer required to delude the unfortunate Métis. Schmidt was convinced that Riel unwillingly was doing the work of Satan.[23] Riel was at war with the clergy while preaching faith and religion to the people. He presented himself as a devout mystic, full of religious airs and this convinced a large number of people that he was nothing less than a saint. These misguided Métis had apostatized themselves to follow him in his heresies. Furthermore, Riel had so deceived the Métis that they believed him to be a veritable prophet and maker of miracles. Schmidt claimed that on the day of the Battle of Batoche Métis women, upon hearing the echo of machine gun fire cried out: "Here is the miracle, listen to the thunder which falls on Middleton's troops". The Métis were convinced that they would win victory after victory and annihilate the Canadian troops.

Schmidt attributed this incredible naiveté to the fact that, instead of heeding the advice of the clergy, the Métis flouted and persecuted them. After the fall of Batoche, Schmidt wrote Taché and stated that Riel had been crushed just in time because more Métis were about to follow him into the horrible abyss of apostasy.[24]

It is ironic to note that Schmidt was such an obscure figure by 1885 that some individuals were able to confuse the part he played in 1870 with developments in the District of Saskatchewan in 1884-85. When the North-West question was being debated in Parliament in July, 1885, M.C. Cameron, the Liberal member for Huron West charged that, in attributing the consequences of the Rebellion to the Liberal party, Sir John A. Macdonald had forgotten to mention the political affiliation of those who had been actively engaged in the movement. Identifying Schmidt as one of the dominant participants, Cameron asked:

> Did he (the Prime Minister) tell us the (political) complexion of Louis Schmidt, a man after his own heart, a man in whom he had such unbounded faith that he appointed him to an office of emolument in the gift of the Crown, a man who I believe still holds that office and, while he was a paid official of the Tory Government, was private secretary and Secretary of State to Louis Riel, the controller of affairs in the great North-West.[25]

Such was Louis Schmidt's brief moment of glory in 1885, if indeed he had one. Fortunately, no legend was created, perpetrated and embellished by future generations.

As a result of his strong orthodox religious and political convictions Schmidt could not become associated with the developments that culminated in open rebellion. The kindest words that Schmidt could find to describe his former classmate and colleague after August, 1884, were "pauvre Riel". The Riel of 1885 was obviously an individual whom he wanted to forget. Louis Schmidt's personal diary for November 16, 1885, contains the following entry: "Le télégraph nous annonce que Riel a été pendu à 10 heures". There are only three other specific references to Riel in fifty-one years of entries and these are one line statements noting the fifth, sixth and twentieth anniversaries of Riel's death.

Since the rebellion was such a hideous aberration in Schmidt's conception of events one finds no retrospective insights in the pages of his diary which might serve to enhance our knowledge of it and the motives of the participants. As a matter of fact, there are very few references, casual or otherwise, to 1885. The entry of July 21, 1901, mentions the unveiling in the Batoche cemetery of a monument to all those who had fallen in the Rebellion. Schmidt simply states that he gave the main address. The entry of September 1, 1905, records a meeting with Gabriel Dumont at Bellevue. Schmidt noted that Dumont had aged considerably but that he still liked to travel and hunt. The entry of May 19, 1906, mentions the death of Gabriel Dumont followed by this simple statement: "Son nom est devenu fameux après la Rébellion de 1885 car c'était le commandement des Métis.''On the same day Schmidt recorded the death of Louis Riel's mother in St. Boniface. It was qualified by the words: "Je l'ai bien connue." On April 28, 1908 Schmidt relates that he was visited by William Henry Jackson and that Jackson took his photograph. On March 26, 1925, there is a reference to the fortieth anniversary of the battle of Duck Lake. The July 9, 1925, entry records the passage of *La Liaison Française,* a group of Quebec visitors, in the nearby town of Hoey. There were speeches and a banquet and Schmidt was surrounded by people who "aiment à connaître le secrétaire de Riel."

After the Liberal victory in 1896, Schmidt was advised that his services would no longer be required at the Lands Office and he returned to his homestead in St. Louis.[26] As a result of his education and experience, Schmidt was a natural candidate for local affairs. In addition to serving as a trustee of the parish, he was secretary of the school district and the rural municipality for many years. In 1912, he participated in the founding convention of l'Association Catholique Franco-Canadienne de la Saskatchewan where he presented an address on the rights of the French language during the territorial era. In 1913, he was selected as one of Saskatchewan's delegates to the first congress of the French language in Quebec city.

Throughout his long life, Louis Schmidt was an intensely religious man who took advantage of every opportunity to practise the precepts of his church. His diary entry for May 22, 1892, reveals his deep religiosity and attachment to the clergy. He referred to that day as "Prince Albert's great day" because it was the blessing of the Cathedral's cornerstone. In the early morning he assisted at part of Bishop Laflèche's mass, all of Bishop Duhamel's and served as assistant for Mgr. Hamel's. Afterwards came breakfast, conversations with numerous clergy and a pontifical high mass. At 2:30 P.M. Archbishop Taché blessed the cornerstone and this was followed by addresses and a sermon. In the evening there were vespers, another sermon and the benediction of the Blessed Sacrament. Today, no one would want to participate in, let along challenge, such a marathon. The fact that Schmidt was a deeply religious man, however, did not make him a slave of the clergy nor did it prevent him from commenting on a clergyman's character and personality. On an extremely cold and windy Sunday morning, for example, Schmidt recorded that the church nearly blew off its foundation adding that this did not prevent the curé from delivering an interminable sermon. On another occasion, he remarked dismally that there were six priests and a French bishop in church but no French sermon.[27]

Louis Schmidt is both a fascinating and interesting character. To begin with, his long life spanned the fur trade, the buffalo hunt, the territorial period and the blossoming of the agricultural frontier. He was an active participant in the events that led to the birth of the province of Manitoba and a keen observer of those that led to the Saskatchewan Rebellion. In addition, he was a literate Métis who as early as the 1860's began to keep a diary or at least rough notes of day to day events. The 61 page manuscript entitled "Notes sur le Mouvement des Métis à St. Laurent (1884)" is a good example of his note keeping. His memoirs published serially in *Le Patriote de l'Ouest* in 1911-12 were obviously written from similar notes. Unfortunately the diary and notes which still exist begin only on October 29, 1885 and continue through April 10, 1934. The pre-1885 notes may very well have been lost in the fire that destroyed *Le Patriote's* printing plant in 1910.

This paper was based upon Schmidt's memoirs, his diary and notes, the 1884 manuscript and his correspondence with Bishop Taché. With additional research, I hope to expand this overview into a more extensive biographical study of Louis Schmidt.

7

A Survey of
Louis Riel's Poetry

Glen Campbell

THREE WEEKS after Louis Riel surrendered at Batoche, the Montreal newspaper *La Minerve* published extracts from three poems that he had written. In a short note preceding the verse, the newspaper states that the "poésies . . . ne sont qu'une partie de celles que l'agitateur se proposait de publier en volume".[1] Although this statement is undoubtedly journalistic speculation, it is probably not too far removed from the truth. On several occasions, Riel expressed the desire to see his poetry in print.[2] To my knowledge, however, he never published any of his works himself. During his lifetime, the only known poems to appear were those which were published in 1870 by his former schoolmate, Eustache Prud'homme in the newspaper *L'Opinion publique*.[3]

In 1886, a few months after Riel's execution, his family published *Poésies Religieuses et Politiques*, a small booklet containing a further eight poems.[4] A certificate, dated January 12, 1886, at St. Vital, and signed by Joseph Riel, Octavie Lavallée, Alexandre Riel and Henriette Poitras, is appended to the booklet and attests to the authenticity of the poetry:

> Nous, membres de la famille Riel, déclarons et certifions que ceci est une vraie copie des documents écrits et composés par Louis "David" Riel.

Since that time, the only major work on the poetry to appear is *Louis Riel: Poésies de jeunesse*, published in 1977 by Gilles Martel, Glen Campbell and Thomas Flanagan.[5]

Riel's total known poetic output, including both draft versions and completed works, comprises approximately 500 manuscript pages. The three main depositories for the poetry are the Public Archives of Canada, the Provincial Archives of Manitoba and the Archives du Séminaire de Québec. Other holdings may be found in the Harriet Irving Library of the University of New Brunswick, the Archives Nationales du Québec, the Séminaire Saint-Joseph de Trois-Rivières, the Bibliothèque du Collège de Lévis, the McCord Museum of McGill University, the Archevêché de Saint-Boniface, the Saskatchewan Archives Board and the R.C.M.P. Museum of Regina.

Riel's poetry consists of political and religious verse as well as songs, fables and love poems. The poems vary in length from 4 to 481 lines, the latter being Riel's extended diatribe against John A. Macdonald and "les Anglais". Approximately eighty percent of the poetry is written in French; the remaining twenty percent is in English. There is one poem "Incendium"[6] composed entirely in Latin. A large part of the verse is autobiographical.

Since poetry is by its very nature self-revelatory, a study of the poetic works should therefore help shed more light on Riel's attitude toward various individuals of historical significance and on incidents in which he was involved. It should equally give us another insight, and perhaps a new perspective on this man who played such a central role in the history of Western Canada. Through the poetry, we can meet Riel, the student priest, Riel the lover, Riel the political activist, the family man, the exiled Canadian. . .

In this overview I have chosen to present the poems, not in a chronological order, but rather according to genres and themes. I think that this method of presentation will allow a greater appreciation of the qualities of Riel the poet and as well, will reveal a more humanistic, sensitive side of the man, a side which often remains hidden in historical reports.

Political themes play a major role in the poetry. There are numerous works concerned with the French Canadians, the Métis and with problems relating to dealings with Ottawa. In one such work (untitled as are many of the poems), Riel speaks of Ottawa's betrayal of his people. The lines have a definite one-sided slant but much of what the poet says about the events in Manitoba of 1869-70 is true.

When the British Parliament passed the Rupert's Land Act in June 1869, allowing the North-West to be sold to Canada, the inhabitants of the region feared the loss of their land. The federal government in its negotiations with the Provisional Government of Riel promised support for separate (i.e.Catholic French) schools as well as for the rights of the native and Métis people to land. This was summed up in the Manitoba Act of May 1870, but the formal declarations were soon forgotten, as Riel deplores in the poem:

> La ville d'outaouais
> Implora de nous la paix
> Et de bouche et d'écriture.

> Son grand désir
> Etait d'adjoindre au sien notre beau territoire
> Sans déplaisir,
> Notre gouvernement n'étant que Provisoire
> Consentit cette union;
> Mais sous la condition
> Qu'on trouve dans notre histoire.
>
> D'un coeur ardent
> Nous avons combattu pour nos droits politiques.
> Dieu nous aidant,
> On nous a garanti tous nos droits catholiques.
> Alors nous sommes entrés
> Parmi les confédérés.
> Mais c'était tous des puniques.[7]

Riel felt a deep personal blow when the "perfidious confederates" reneged on their promises. He had dealt honorably with Ottawa, he states, but it has, in turn, treated him like dirt:

> Mes droits chrétiens
> Le monde d'Ottawa les a mis dans la boue.
> Moi qui soutiens
> La justice et l'honneur, Ottawa me baffoue.
> Dieu veut que j'en donne avis:
> Par le christ en qui je vis,
> Il faut que l'erreur échoue.[8]

Riel epitomizes many of the problems inherent in Canada's history: the problems between the English and the French, the Natives and the Whites, the East and the West. Regardless of the conflict, Riel always represents the underdog, and his poetry is clearly indicative of this point of view. Of all the problems about which he writes, it is the English-French struggle which appears the most often in his verse. In one poem, he speaks about the relationship of the two linguistic groups in Quebec:

> Dans le Bas Canada, la classe gouvernante
> Dit généralement qu'elle est fière et contente
> D'obéir à l'anglais; qu'il est pour nous, courtois
> Et bon de nous laisser faire nos propres lois.[9]

If such an arrangement appears, on the surface, to be harmonious, Riel goes on to explain the reason underlying this state of affairs. At the same time, he criticizes the servility of his own people:

Mois je sais qu l'Anglais ne fera pas d'outrage
Aux canadiens français qui font bien son ouvrage.
L'Anglais est égoîste et plein d'ambition
Chaque fois qu'il rencontre un instrument docile
Il s'en sert et le traite avec précaution.
Surtout s'ils s'aperçoit que son homme est servile.[10]

Although Riel's mistrust of "l'Anglais" continued throughout his life, he could, when the occasion demanded, produce poetry that gave quite another impression. A political about-face is noted in one such poem which was written while Riel was awaiting trial in Regina. The lines, dated July 12, 1885, are dedicated to Captain Dean, Commander of the Mounted Police:

Béni soit Dieu qui glorifie
Le règne de Victoria!. . .
Qu'elle aime, mais sans préférence,
Le peuple canadien-français.
Que toute la Nouvelle France
Trouve auprès d'Elle un libre accès.

Sous son admirable couronne
Sous son règne majestueux,
Puissante race anglo-saxonne
Rendez les irlandais heureux!

Que Jésus le Fils de Dieu même
Fasse étinceler sur les Mers
Et les terres, le diadème
De la Reine, dans l'univers.[11]

What better way to gain the favour of the Head Jailer than to praise his mother country and Queen! There is no doubt that Riel knew how to combine his poetic and political talents.

The French-speaking Métis provide the theme for several of the poetic creations. Riel speaks openly, often candidly, about the new racial group which has been created on Canadian soil, the group of which he is one. In an extract from an ode to the French-Canadian Métis, composed in August, 1883, the poet talks about the great future in store for his people, that is, if its three composite elements blend together well:

J'aime sans mesure et j'admire
Les Métis-canadiens-français:
Ce peuple nouveau qui se mire
Déjà dans de brillants succès. . .

Métis et Canadiens ensemble
Français, si nos trois éléments
S'amalgament bien, il me semble
Que nous serons un jour plus grands.[12]

In a similar poem, Riel tells us how in the "three-blooded race", the good qualities of one race hold in check the bad qualities of another. Then, while stating the essential character of each, he attempts to determine which of the three, the *Français,* the *Canadien* or the *Métis*, has done the most good:

Les bonnes qualités canadiennes-françaises
Corrigent les défauts de notre sang indien.
Ainsi par les vertus avez-vous quelques aises
A tenir en échec les qualités mauvaises
Dans la race à trois sangs. Est-ce le canadien,
Est-ce le français ou le Métis dont l'exemple
Mérite plus qu'on le contemple?
Quel est celui des trois qui fait le plus de bien?

Le Métis est charitable,
Et le canadien traitable
Le bon français a vieilli
A défendre l'église. Elle est belle sa page
D'histoire! Il faut qu'il propage
Sa foi qui n'a pas failli.[13]

The survival of the French and Métis in the midst of an English-speaking majority is a recurrent theme in Riel's verse. The possible assimilation, even annihilation of the minorities are grave concerns of the poet. There is, however, one specific aspect of the anglophone menace which obsesses him. This obsession is embodied in the person of Sir John A. Macdonald. Not only does Macdonald incarnate all the wrongs of the Anglo-Saxon race, according to Riel, but he is regarded as a bitter personal enemy.

After the Thomas Scott affair, the Macdonald government had promised a general amnesty to all those involved. Riel, however, was excluded from this pardon and never forgave Macdonald for breaking his word. He was later granted amnesty by the Mackenzie government on the condition that he exile himself from Canada for five years. During his exile in the United States, Riel used his creative talents to launch a scathing attack against the Canadian politician. The following are the opening lines of this poetic vendetta:

Sir John A. MacDonald gouverne avec orgueil
Les provinces de la Puissance
Et sa mauvaise foi veut prolonger mon deuil
Afin que son pays l'applaudisse et l'encense.

> Au lieu de la paix qu'il me doit;
> Au lieu de respecter d'une manière exacte
> Notre Pacte
> Et mon droit,
> Depuis bientôt six ans, Sir John me fait la guerre.
> Un homme sans parole est un homme vulgaire,
> Fort ou faible d'esprit, moi, je le montre au doigt.[14]

Riel's resentment against his political enemies festered during the time he spent in the United States. He pondered his condition; he conjectured about his destiny. Many of these innermost thoughts are preserved in the poetry. The real reason for his banishment, as he declares in one of his poems, is that "les anglais" feared his genius. What they "stole" from the world will, however, be restored. With God's help, he will arise again and succeed: he is another Lafayette:

> Les anglais ont craint mon génie
> Ils m'ont coupé chemin partout
> Ma personne qu'ils ont bannie
> Surgit et veut rester debout.
>
> Si mon Dieu le veut, s'il me prête
> La force, je réussirai.
> Je suis un autre Lafayette.
> J'irai loin: je sais où j'irai.
>
> Les Etats-Unis me reçoivent
> Les anglais n'auront pas pour rien
> Ce qu'ils ont volé, ce qu'ils doivent
> Au monde; je suis citoyen.[15]

There is no doubt that Riel was a man of great vision. It is unfortunate for him that he often neglected the everyday, down-to-earth, practical matters which were necessary to turn his dreams into reality.

The autobiographical nature of much of the poetry has helped us piece together a more complete picture of Riel's life and has given us a greater understanding of his beliefs, attitudes and feelings. We know, for instance, how he felt about being sent to study at the Sulpician seminary in Montreal. Even though it meant leaving his family, he was delighted at having been chosen by the Bishop of Saint-Boniface, Alexandre Taché. Riel never forgot what Taché had done for him and often referred to him in grateful terms in his verse:

> Si ma poésie est l'oeuvre de bon poète
> Je l'offre à votre grâce; et j'en ai du plaisir.

Ma langue, Monseigneur, serait presque muette
Si vous ne m'aviez pas aimé pour me choisir
Comme vous l'aviez fait d'une manière aimable
Lorsque j'avais douze ans.
Je me souviens toujours de quel air agréable
Vous m'avez désigné parmi beaucoup d'enfants,
En disant: Nous pourrions, je crois, le faire instruire.
O dix-huit cent cinquante-huit.
A mes yeux charmés, c'est Dieu qui vous a fait luire!
Vous êtes l'année où, jeune, l'on m'a conduit
Dans le noble pays de la Nouvelle France
Pour me sauver de l'ignorance
Et des profondeurs de sa nuit!

Grâce à vous, Monseigneur, j'eus ma place au collège
Des Sulpiciens de Montréal.
J'eus l'éducation qu'approuve le Saint Siège.
Et ma jeunesse a vu clair . . .[16]

In another version of the poem, the "Father of Manitoba" expresses his gratitude to his benefactor and states that had it not been for Taché, he would not have had the glory of founding the province, of establishing the constitution of Manitoba, his dearly-beloved native land:

Ah! si vous n'aviez pas été mon protecteur!
Ah! si vous n'aviez pas été mon bienfaiteur
Je n'aurais jamais eu la gloire de construire
La fortification
De la constitution
Du Manitoba ma patrie:
Ma place natale chérie![17]

When the young Louis was living in Montreal, he copied into a small exercise-book three dozen poems that he had composed.[18] Two-thirds of them are written in the form of fables, based on the style of La Fontaine. It is possible that some of these were composed for class assignments, and Riel's taste being whetted, he continued to write them for his own pleasure. The moralizing inherent in the fable genre obviously appealed to his vision of the world in which all was black and white, where good and evil existed but where vice was always punished, virtue always rewarded.

In the fable entitled "La Souris" we have a pleasing departure from this rather sterile concept of the world. Although there is some moralizing, the fable is more of a commentary on the conduct of parliamentarians of Riel's time. We can speculate that it was written after young Riel had attended a sitting of Parliament and was shocked by what he saw there:

Une souris entra dans un appartement
Où se tenait le Parlement.
A l'aspect de cette assemblée
Elle se sentit troublée.
Et fut un gros quart'heure à reprendre ses sens.
Tant elle eut peur de ces gens.
Non qu'ils eussent un air trop grave, trop austère;
Mais bien de les trouver tous remplis de colère.
Elle se mit dans un coin
Dans le fond d'une issue, et regarda de loin.
S'accordant mal entr'eux, ils se portaient de rage
Les poings au visage.
Jurons surannés
Correspondaient partout aux mots les mieux donnés
C'était du tapage.
Enfin toutes les gens s'étaient abandonnés.
Jugeons si la souris s'en revint étonnée.
Elle parla
De tout cela
A sa mère par qui souvent notre lignée
A propos de sagesse, avait été prônée.
Mais seraient-ce bien là ces hommes si vantés?
Disait-elle; prudents; de tant de qualités?
Ceux-là pourtant devaient avoir quelle sagesse
Si le commandement convient à la noblesse.
Que penser des sujets
Si tels sont les préfets?
Même parmi, j'ai vu plus d'une barbe grise;
Appuya-t-elle enfin dans sa grande surprise.
S'il est vrai que ces gens font de pareils excès
S'ils sont ce que tu dis, lui répartit la mère
La conclusion est que l'homme dégénère.[19]

It would seem that some of the mouse's observations would not be too far removed from the truth today.

One of the non-fable poems of the notebook, and one of Riel's more successful poetic efforts, is entitled "Le Serpent". It brings to mind some of the compositions of Leconte de Lisle, the French Parnassian poet of the mid-nineteenth century. The imprint of the French Romantic poets is also apparent, as we see the reptile at odds with his fate. We see his anxiety, his suffering as he meditates on the "divine curse" which crushes him:

Les yeux toujours ardents, il va, circule, avance,
S'inquiète de tout et même du silence.
Le ciel qui l'a maudit l'empêche de jouir.
A le voir se traîner il a l'air de souffrir.

Il se tord en tous sens. Replié sur lui-même
Ecrasé sous le poids du divin anathème,
Soigneux à nous cacher l'opprobre de son sort
Ne semblerait-il pas qu'il nourrit un remords?
Dans sa marche pénible on croirait qu'il médite,
Qu'il souffre des affronts de sa race maudite.[20]

It is interesting to note that in Riel's youthful verse composed in Montreal, there is no poem specificaly devoted to the Métis, to the Indians. . . no open reference to his racial origins. I do, however, feel that Riel, who was for all intents and purposes French-Canadian (he only had 1/8 Indian blood), was sensitive at that time to his Métis extraction. This sensitivity appears unconsciously, I believe, in several of the early poems where Riel uses terms similar to the expression ''race maudite'' found in the lines cited above. In this light, the ''Snake'' is possibly a transfiguration of the poet. The spiritual anguish of the reptile is really that of the young Métis, alienated in Montreal, far from the wild prairie of his childhood. The poet is perhaps unconsciously expressing concern about his ancestral differences, about the humiliation and dispair caused by racial prejudice.[21]

It was not until Riel had returned to his homeland and had adopted the cause of the Métis people that his mixed blood became a source of intense pride for him, and, as a direct consequence, an important theme of his poetry. In several compositions, he glorifies his ancestors, both French and Indian. Here is one in which his mother's side of the family is singled out for praise:

Le Manitoba se fait glorie
De notre nom, ô mes aieux.
Il est écrit dans son histoire
En caractères lumineux.

Ma mère est de race guerrière
Elle vient du pur sang français.
Et Louis, nom de la Gimodière
Est illustre, ancien, je le sais.

Ce nom est écrit sur le bronze.
Le ciel a voulu l'éprouver.
Me mère est du sang de Louis Onze
La chose est facile à trouver.[22]

In spite of the small amount of Indian blood flowing in his veins, Riel exploited to the fullest this ancestral fact, and ultimately adopted the Métis and native people's cause as his own. Here are a few lines from another poem in which his paternal forebears are glorified:

Le Sang Sauvage en moi rayonne;
Et je louange mes aieux.
Vous m'avez chanté la Huronne
Sur le ton le plus gracieux.
Il vous a plu de reconnaître
Son air encor fier et charmant.
Poète, j'ai dû vous promettre
Mes chants en guise de payement.[23]

As far as Riel's romantic interests are concerned, there appear to have been three women in his life. As one might expect from someone with poetic tendencies, Louis put pen to paper and recorded for posterity the thoughts that these romances inspired.

Extracts from these compositions will help reveal the sentimental Riel. The first, entitled "Un Jeune Malade", is a song from a dying man to the girl he loves. The setting is autumn, and the young man, like Nature, is brought closer to his death with each leaf that falls. The theme is by no means original but Riel who was about 20 years of age when he wrote it, treats it with sensitivity:

Voici le sombre automne
Avec ses vents de froid
Qui, d'un cri monotone
Soupirent avec moi.
La nature est mourante
Quand viennent les frimas
Et ma force expirante
Me parle du trépas!

Adieu, tendre verdure
De nos joyeux bosquets!
La bise et la froidure
Flétrissent tes attraits!
Aussi moi, je succombe.
Je ne te survis pas.
Chaque feuille qui tombe
M'annonce le trépas.

Privés du doux feuillage
Les oiseaux de nos bois
Sur un autre rivage
Font entendre leur voix.
Ici, plus d'allégresse!
Le deuil est sous mes pas.
Et le mal qui m'oppresse
M'apporte le trépas.

O toi que j'ai chérie,
Quand j'aurai clos mes yeux
Fidèle et tendre amie!
Souviens-toi de nos voeux!
Quelquefois sur ma cendre
Doubliant tes appas
Viens te faire entendre
Et plaindre mon trépas![24]

If we consider the poem as autobiographical, the girl in question is probably Marie-Julie Guernon, the young Montreal girl Riel wished to marry. The imminent death would therefore be spiritual, not physical, and refer to the relationship between the two lovers. Since we are not certain of the actual date of composition of the poem, there are two possible explanations for the "mal" which oppresses the poet. It could be the moral dilemma faced by the young man who has chosen to continue his studies for the priesthood rather than to pursue the amorous alliance. The other possibility which would explain the symbolic death is the refusal of the Guernon family to allow Riel to marry their daughter.

Riel's second romantic involvement was with Evelina Barnabé, sister of Father Fabien Barnabé, pastor of the church in Keeseville, New York. Louis had stayed with the Barnabé family on several occasions. During one of his visits, he became secretly engaged to Evelina.[25] In a poem addressed to the young woman in April, 1878, Riel explains the reasons for his marriage proposal. He worships her, he says, because she is a righteous woman of exemplary character and inspired heart. The poet implies that he, by contrast, is a rather lowly person who needs Evelina's goodness and godliness to help him overcome various moral difficulties:

Je demande au bon Dieu qu'il exauce mes voeux
En daignant nous unir, au plus tôt, tous les deux.
Oh! si vous souhaitez fonder une famille
Qui soit capable un jour de lutter pour le bien,
J'aime à vous rechercher; car vous êtes la fille
Dont le coeur inspiré peut comprendre le mien.

Plus votre vie est exemplaire,
Plus aussi savez-vous me plaire.
Moi, je suis un homme de rien.
Je vaux à peine un peu de boue.
Je crains qu'au moindre choc ma vertu ne s'échoue;
Mais pour m'aider, je cherche une femme de bien.[26]

Although the two corresponded for some months after Riel's departure for the

Western United States, the marriage never took place. It is thought that the frail health of Evelina would very likely not have withstood the rigours of life in the West. Perhaps Riel felt that his economic instability would not have allowed him to provide a decent home for her.[27] At any rate, the two never saw one another again.

While he was in Montana, the lonely Riel, in 1881, married Marguertie Monette, a Cree-speaking Métisse who knew little French or English. Since there was no priest in the vicinity, the two contracted what is known as a "prairie marriage", i.e. they agreed to live common-law until such time as their union could be sanctified by the church.[28] Riel tells us in a poem that his relationship with Margeurite had been divinely inspired. He had prayed for fifteen years, he declares, for God to choose the right girl for him and is convinced that he has now found her:

> J'ai prié durant quinze années
> Le Tout Puissant de me choisir
> Parmi les filles les mieux nées
> Une femme de bon désir . . .
> Oui, j'ai trouvé selon mes voeux
> Le sujet de mon allégresse
> La femme même que je veux.[29]

It would appear from the poem that Marguerite had misgivings about the common-law arrangement. Riel attempts to convince her of the sancitity of their union:

> Je vis avec vous, ma promise
> Mais je ne vous ai pas encore
> Mariée en face de l'église.
> Mais vous avez mon anneau d'or.
>
> Je vous ai mariée ô ma fille
> En dix-huit cent quatre-vingt-un.
> Au désert, près de la coquille
> Devant Dieu par le droit commun.
>
> Aussitôt que viendra le prêtre
> Nous nous rendrons ensemble à lui
> Nous irons rencontrer peut-être
> Jusqu'à Benton, son saint appui . . .
>
> C'est la longue absence du Prêtre
> Ma fille, qui nous a contraints
> De nous marier ainsi.
>
> Ma fille, vous n'aurez pas honte.[30]

Since the young Métisse could neither read nor write, one wonders, after reading these lines, if it was not only Marguerite that the deeply-religious Riel was trying to convince!

Two months before the birth of their son, Jean, in May 1882, a priest, Father Joseph Damiani arrived and solemnized their marriage. The couple's second child, Marie-Angélique was born the following year.[31] Riel's political activities were all encompassing, and it appears that even at the best of times he was not a good provider. When he was imprisoned, things became even worse for his family. In a poem, dated June, 1885, and addressed to the Commanding Officer of the Mounted Police in Regina, he makes an impassioned plea for Marguerite and the children:

> Would the governor
> And the government
> Grant me a favor
> In my detainment?
> My wife, my children
> Are poor, have no bread.
> Could I use my pen
> In Jail, for their aid?. . .
>
> Ah! perhaps your press
> And your volunteers
> Would, in my distress,
> Buy my reading tears!
> I would, with the price,
> Get for my children,
> Half a cup of rice
> Or half a chicken. . .
>
> Some bread, for my wife
> My dear Margaret:
> And spare her a strife
> With want and regret.[32]

While awaiting the hangman, Riel penned a good deal of verse most of which was destined for his family and friends. The prevailing tone of these compositions is religious. Here are excerpts from prayers for his children:

> Priez Jésus Marie en faveur de mon Sang,
> Pour mes petits enfants, pour mon fils et ma fille.
> Soyez le gardien fort de leur coeur innocent.
> O Saint Joseph! Priez pour toute ma famille.
>
> Priez Dieu, s'il vous plaît, pour Jean mon fils aîné.
> Si telle est du Seigneur la volonté parfaite,

Qu'il vive de longs jours, qu'il soit homme de tête,
Sobre, frugal, discret, toujours bien ordonné.[33]

Priez notre Seigneur d'exaucer ma supplique;
S'il lui plaît; de me conserver
Ma fille Marie-Angélique:
Qu'il m'aide à la bien élever
Au bon lait, au pain frais de la foi catholique.[34]

In general, the verse that Riel composed in English does not rise to any great heights. This is quite understandable but even if the English poetry lacks eloquence, some of the lines do however contain a fair amount of wisdom, as in this example:

But politics are hot a ground
Where the roots of passions grow deep.
One has to be well back'd up, sound
To walk there and get away cheap.[35]

The following lines offer a succinct assertion of Riel's belief:

Without wish to oppose
Those
Who believe other wise,
I give it as a fact
Mary Immaculate.[36]

Here is an amusing verse from another peom in which the rhyming also leaves something to be desired:

I can sing the fair amazone
With her long dress on the saddle;
And whisper as the telephone
Tunes to babies in their cradle.[37]

Occasionally, even in French, some of Riel's verses are unintentionally comical as in this love poem to Evelina Barnabé:

Les lèvres de ma bien-aimée
Tentent ma bouche encore plus que le melon d'eau
Quand j'ai soif. . .[38]

Obviously not finding the lines completely satisfactory, Riel rewrote them:

Je trouve les baisers de sa bouche, aussi frais
Que la chair et le jus du bon melon français.[39]

It is interesting to note how, in the revised version, the melon takes on certain nationalistic overtones!

From a literary point of view, it is evident that Riel's verse does not constitute what one would call "great poetry". Technically, the verse is good. The poet shows a solid mastery of the art of versification. What is lacking the most often is inspiration, and this is of course the essential criterion which distinguishes a versemonger from a true poet. The poetry composed in Riel's younger years shows certain touches of this quality; the later works, being more utilitarian in purpose, are generally inferior. They lack the intensity and feeling which can be found in some of the earlier compositions, such as the letters in verse written to George Etienne Cartier. These epistolary poems, written to Cartier in 1886, constitute some of Riel's more successful poetic efforts. The young Louis makes a lyrical request for employment and implores the politician to help him. Idleness is gnawing away at him. His future looks bleak. The empty hours only add to his solitude; he is reduced to living on hope:

> . . . Je ne suis rien! Je languis et j'attends!
> La triste oisiveté consume tout mon temps.
> Et que puis-je? Ignoré, sans aucune assistance
> Désoeuvré, seul, réduit à vivre d'espérance?[40]

Riel's despair is evident and his lines touch us by their profound sincerity. The portrait that he paints of himself is moving, often pathetic. When his earlier request falls on deaf ears, the poet becomes more impatient, more discouraged and he finds himself filled with a profound *ennui*:

> Dans les profonds ennuis d'un noir isolement
> Je médite le deuil qui couvre ma jeunesse.
> Et la douleur m'oppresse!
> Comme des glas, je sens, de funèbres concerts
> S'agiter dans mon sein chargé de pleurs amers!
> Ferais-je retentir le cri de ma détresse?
> Sous la fatalité, qui me poursuit sans cesse
> Trouverai-je un écho dans ces mornes déserts
> De la noire infortune à qui mes maux sont chers?. . .
> C'est en vain que ma plainte
> Fatiguerait le ciel d'une voix presqu'éteinte![41]

The lyrical impulses, the sentimental outpourings and the rich imagery of these lines are evidence that a great deal of time and effort was spent in their creation. Had the poet devoted the same amount of energy to his later endeavours, it is quite possible that his verse could have occupied a more noteworthy place in Canadian literature. As it is, the poetry does, at least from a biographical perspective, have a definite value since it allows a revealing and penetrating view of the more intimate side of our enigmatic historical figure.

8

The Political Thought of Louis Riel

Thomas Flanagan

LOUIS RIEL was not a political theorist in any usual sense of the term. He never pondered systematically on the great questions of man and the state. But he was a man to whom ideas were supremely important, and his political actions were always influenced by deeply held convictions. Thus it is appropriate to discuss his "political thought", if not his "political theory", just as one might discuss the political thought of Laurier, Macdonald, or other leading Canadian politicians. Such a discussion of Riel is worthwhile because of his historical importance and because of the intrinsic interest of his position as a spokesman for racial minorities. The latter point is especially relevant today when questions of language and native rights are so hotly contested.

It is impossible to give a single definitive outline of Riel's ideas, for his views changed often and went through several distinct phases. Thus I have adopted the following procedure: First I give a brief sketch of his intellectual development, indicating some of the influences to which he was subject and pointing out the broad stages in his thinking. Then I single out for discussion three themes with which Riel was concerned during all or most of these stages: nationalism, native rights, and the relationship of religious to secular authority.

Intellectual Development
Riel studied with the Sulpician Fathers at the College of Montreal from 1858 to 1865, stopping just short of his baccalaureate. He received a thorough groun-

ding in classical languages, French literature, philosophy, and theology.

His first hero seems to have been Sir G.E. Cartier. After he left the College, he wrote three epistolary poems to Cartier asking for employment.[1] There is little trace of his political views in these poems except that, like Cartier, he was for Confederation. But when Cartier did not find him a job, Riel went to study law with Rodolphe Laflamme, a leading *rouge*. It is not known whether his outlook changed correspondingly.

The events of 1869/70 thrust Riel into the leadership of the Métis of Red River. He did not yet have a very elaborate set of political ideas beyond the determination to defend the interests of his people. He was under two rather conflicting sorts of influence. On the one hand, the logic of the situation, plus the presence of American advisers, pushed him in the direction of the frontier democracy analyzed by S. D. Clark.[2] Thus Riel wrote declarations of rights and bills of grievances, organized committees of public safety, declared local autonomy, and so forth. It all seemed quite radical. But on the other hand, Riel was also close to the missionary clergy, especially Fathers Ritchot and Dugas, who were militant in defending the French language and Catholic religion, but were far from radical in other respects. These conflicting pressures produced such curious results as the Declaration of the First Provisional Government of December 8, 1869, in which Riel defended the Métis cause with arguments drawn from the sixteenth-century Gallican absolutist William Barclay.[3]

Riel's thinking did not undergo any particular change for about three years after the "Rebellion". He was chiefly concerned to obtain an amnesty for himself, and punctilious fulfilment of the Manitoba Act for the Métis. But a decisive shift in his thought began in early 1874, after he had gone east to press his case. He was in constant contact there with the ultramontane school of Quebec politics. Alphonse Desjardins, editor of the *Nouveau Monde*, became his confidant. Riel also developed a close relationship with Ignace Bourget, Bishop of Montreal and the leading ultra. Another mentor was Bishop Laflèche of Trois-Rivières, who as a missionary had been one of Riel's first teachers in Red River. Riel now absorbed the leading ideas of the Quebec ultras: loyalty to the the pope (including the doctrine of papal infallibility), control of the state by the church, ecclesiastical intervention in party politics and the special religious mission of the French-Canadian nation. In taking over this latter notion, Riel modified it somewhat to create a special niche for the Métis, who would become a "sacerdotal people" like the French-Canadians.

Failure to achieve his political goals led Riel to take more and more consolation in religion. He began to see his reverses as providential sufferings ordained by God to purify him and make him worthy to lead the Métis to glory. On December 8, 1875, he underwent an unusual experience of mystical illumination while visiting a friend in Washington, D.C. He thereafter began to call himself the "Prophet of the New World" and to preach an exaggerated ultramontanism in which the role of the Métis eclipsed that of the French-Canadians.

His friends and family interpreted his religious inspiration as insanity. After a period of private arrest, he was confined to lunatic asylums in the province of Quebec from March 6, 1876, to January 23, 1878. He created there a new religion of which he was the inspired prophet. He broke with Rome and transferred papal power to Mgr. Bourget. The Métis were declared a new Chosen People in imitation of the Hebrews. They were to revive selected aspects of the Mosaic Law, including circumcision, the Saturday Sabbath, a married clergy, and polygamy. The papacy would eventually come to rest among the Métis in the village of St. Vital, Riel's home. The pope would be there, ruling the peoples of the earth in theocratic splendour, when Christ returned to earth in the Second Coming. Riel called his new religion "the Catholic, Apostolic, and Vital Church of the Shining Mountains" (*église catholique, apostolique et vitale des Montagnes Lumineuses:* a pun on St. Vital).

Riel was bound to be considered insane as long as he maintained such doctrines. He did eventually gain his freedom by recanting and admitting that he had been temporarily mad. It is difficult to say whether the "cure" was genuine or feigned. At all events, it can be shown that Riel was having visions again within a month of his release from hospital.[4]

Discharge began a long interregnum in his life. He sought work unsuccessfully in New York City. Equally unsuccessfully he tried to interest the New York Fenians in an invasion of Western Canada. He went to Minnesota in late 1878. In the summer of 1879 he went to Montana, where he tried to form an Indian coalition to invade Canada. This came to naught, so Riel roamed Montana with the Métis for several years, supporting himself as a petty trader. During this period he tried to get the American government to grant the Métis a reservation, but this project also failed. Gradually Riel began to sink roots in Montana. He involved himself in local politics and became an American citizen. He married, fathered children, and settled down as a teacher in a mission school run by the Jesuits. He was there when Gabriel Dumont and three others arrived in early June, 1884, to invite him to come to the valley of the Saskatchewan.

All these years Riel was, to external appearances, a loyal and orthodox Catholic. But his private papers show that he still clung to the novel beliefs he had developed in the years 1876-78. The chief difference was that he now believed his mission was to wait until God gave some visible and dramatic sign for him to begin preaching in public. The Catholic Church would retain provisional validity until that moment.

The major addition to Riel's thinking in this period was a new interest in immigration. Through Father Fabien Barnabé of Keeseville, New York, he learned about Bishop John Ireland's Catholic Colonization Bureau. Riel became fascinated with the idea of bringing Catholic immigrants to the West to start a new life. He wanted not only French and French-Canadians to bolster the Métis presence, but many other nationalities as well.

I will not say much about the well-known events of the North-West Rebellion. It is enough to note that Riel did not come to Canada to start a rebellion. He pursued a constitutional path of agitation for many months, and only charted a rebellious course when it became apparent that he would fail in his private goal of getting money for himself from the Canadian government. The Rebellion itself was both a political and a religious movement. Riel unveiled his new church to the world, and most of the Métis of Batoche became converts.

For some years Riel's thinking had been moving in an ecumenical direction, evidenced by his sweeping immigration plans. There were even traces of this spirit in the Rebellion, though they were difficult to see in what appeared from the outside to be a narrow, sectional movement of the Métis. Riel's ecumenism blossomed after his defeat and surrender. He modified his religion to make it appeal to Protestants as well as Catholics. He pleaded for racial and religious reconcilliation at his trial.

Riel was convicted of high treason and sentenced to death on August 1, 1885. The shock temporarily broke his spirit of independence, and he reentered the Catholic Church after signing an abjuration of his heresies. But the retraction was only exterior. He quickly began to experience revelations again. In the solitude of his cell, his concerns expanded to encompass all peoples and races. He made diary entries concerning Latin America and Europe. He sketched out utopian political and religious schemes of world reform. To the last, he hoped that his new religion would be established, the Métis would be vindicated, and world peace would be established.

His mission even extended beyond the grave. Riel went to the scaffold on November 16 expecting that he, like Christ, would be resurrected on the third day.[5]

Nationalism

Louis Riel was a nationalist thinker in two important ways:

(1) He considered the Métis of Western Canada to be a distinct people or nation held together by objective ties of race, language, and religion, and by a subjective sense of belongingness. The Métis were not simply another tribe of natives, nor were they an appendage of the French-Canadian people. They were a new nation in the West, similar except in numbers to the French, Spanish, Polish, or other well-established nations.

Note that Métis in this context refers only to the French-speaking element of the Western half-breeds. These were Riel's people. The English-speaking half-breeds were relatives, but not part of the same nation. The modern Canadian usage of "Métis" to denote all half-breeds, whatever their mother tongue, is a euphemism which seems to date from the early 1940's and was unknown in Riel's time.

(2) The Métis nation was the central concept of Riel's thought and the focus of his life's work. All his plans, both religious and political, were meant to advance the interests of the Métis. This nationalism did not rest on the narrow dogma that the nation must become a nation-state. At all times, Riel wanted to shelter the small Métis nation within some larger political structure. His thinking about the proper structure often changed, but the underlying intention was stable.

Riel's determination to establish the Métis as a distinct Francophone nation in North America suggests a comparison with his contemporary, Pierre Landry, father of the Acadian Renaissance. Both asserted the separateness of their peoples from the French-Canadians; both wanted to protect their peoples in a multi-national structure.

Riel did not create Métis nationalism. A well-established, if somewhat vague tradition already existed.[6] Since the days of the trade war between the Hudson's Bay Company and the Northwest Company, the Métis had been known to call themselves the "new nation".

Riel was exposed to this tradition as a child, but then went at age fourteen to the College of Montreal. His youthful thinking is chiefly known to us from a notebook of poetry composed when he was around twenty. These poems suggest more of French-Canadian nationalism than a specifically Métis feeling. One poem, written in Latin, describes the great fire of Montreal of June 7, 1852. The text reproaches the British garrison of the Ile Ste-Hélène for not helping fight the fire.[7] Another poem, entitled "Le Chat et les Souris", is modeled on a fable by La Fontaine. The cat is described as "anglais par la naissance", a "Saxon", "un lord sans pitié". The oppressed mice unite their forces and overthrow the cat, thus finally tasting "les joies de la vengeance".[8] The moral of the story is so clear that it hardly needs comment.

W.L.Morton has argued that an explanation of the Red River uprising must be sought in the "sense of nationhood of the Métis".[9] Although this may well be true, one will not find many public statements by Riel or other Métis leaders reflecting this specific nationalism. Riel did go so far as to name his newspaper *The New Nation*, but beyond that he was most cautious. The logic of the situation demanded that the Métis seek the support or at least the benign neutrality of the English half-breeds and white settlers. There was little hope of gaining concessions from Canada if the Colony was openly divided. Thus his speeches and manifestos were always addressed to the people of Red River or the North West, not the Métis nation narrowly defined. He spoke for the alleged rights of all settlers (excluding the Indians, who were not part of the movement).

An interesting example of Riel's caution is found in the "Declaration of the People of Rupert's Land and the North West", December 8, 1869, which established the first Provisional Government. The original French text, written in the hand of Father Dugas, stated that the "population actuelle" was now advanced enough to deserve "une place parmi les *nations*". The last word was strongly underlined. But the statement was changed in the printed version to the much milder wording that the "population . . . commands a place amongst the Colonies".[10] Riel was apparently reluctant to use nationalist rhetoric which might prove divisive.

Riel wanted the Colony to enter Confederation as a province with institutions modeled on those of Quebec: local control of land and natural resources, responsible government, a bilingual Governor, bilingualism in the legislature and courts, and a tax-supported system of Protestant and Catholic schools. Beyond this he made no public claims of special protection for the Métis except for a land grant, which would apply to English half-breeds as well. He did privately instruct his envoy to Ottawa, Father Ritchot, to "demand that the country be divided in two, so that the custom of two populations living separately may be maintained. . .and for the protection of those of our rights which are most threatened".[11] But Riel did not seem downcast that nothing came of this idea. He apparently believed the Métis would be sufficiently protected in a province which was a Western replica of Quebec.

Riel's political reverses after 1870 made him dependent upon the Quebec supporters of the Métis. This, plus his close contact with the ultramontanes, encouraged him at least for a while, to think of the Métis as little more than a branch of the French-Canadians. On June 24, 1874, he wrote to the President of the Saint Jean-Baptiste Society of Montreal:

> The French-Canadian Métis of the North (West) are a branch of the French-Canadian tree. They want to grow like that tree, with that tree; they never want to be separated from it, they want to suffer and rejoice with it.[12]

Later that year he wrote to Father Ritchot that it was necessary to obtain "a good piece of land" for the Métis to preserve "this small people" and their Métis identity. This sounds like Métis nationalism; but, continued Riel, it was necessary to encourage French-Canadian immigration to Manitoba, not only to bolster the numbers of the Métis but to help them adopt

> more French-Canadian customs and traditions, so that while we call ourselves the Métis people, we may become in fact assimilated to the province of Quebec through education—without effort or recalcitrance.[13]

Riel was not long content with this submissive attitude. His Métis nationalism grew as his ultramontanism developed a more personal flavour. On December 6, 1875, he asked Mgr. Bourget to notify the pope that "a new Catholic people is arising now in the world: the Métis people". The pope would be consoled if he knew how "the political leaders of this little people have the ambition of

making them a truly Catholic people. . ." Bourget was to write as follows to
the Pope:

> Holy Father, bless the Métis nation. They are the youngest of all the nations of
> the world. They are so small. They love the Blessed Virgin. Bless them as Catholic
> nation. And the Métis nation will be your joy amid your family composed of all
> the other peoples.[14]

Once Riel became a full-fledged prophet and religious founder, the Métis
assumed a correlative position as Chosen People of the modern age. They
would be called upon to complete the work of evangelizing the New World,
begun but not completed by France and the French-Canadians. Riel wrote to
one of his cousins:

> The French-Canadian nation has received from God the wonderful mission of
> continuing the great works of France on this side of the ocean...When the
> French-Canadian nation will have done its work and will be afflicted with the in-
> firmities of old age, its mission must pass to other hands . . . We are working to
> make the French-Canadian Métis people sufficiently great to be worthy to receive
> the heritage of Lower Canada. . .[15]

This text presents a picture of smooth transition from the French-Canadian
mission to that of the Métis. However, Riel makes it clear elsewhere that the
French-Canadians have sinned and the Conquest was their punishment for
failing to fulfill their mission properly. They will receive another chance for
glory now that Mgr. Bourget has been made pope, as of December 8, 1875.
But in the future they will again fall prey to the temptations of "liberalism".
The Holy Spirit will not find an adequate instrument until the Métis become
the "sacerdotal people" and the papacy flees from Montreal to St. Vital (in
the year 2333 A.D.).[16]

The Métis were descended on their mothers' side from the Indians, who in
turn were descendants of Jews who had come to America about the time of
Moses. This was revealed to Riel in copious detail, which he communicated to
Mgr. Bourget.[17] Thus it was appropriate to revive the Mosaic Law for the New
Chosen People, who were tied not only symbolically but genealogically to the
old.

This notion of a glorious hidden ancestry is a common aspect of many
millenarian forms of nativism. It can be compared to the assertion of the Black
Muslims that they are not Negroes but the "lost-found nation of Islam", or of
the Jamaican Rastafarians that they are really Ethiopians. It is a way of digni-
fying the new Chosen People and justifying their glorious future.

Riel's nationalism reached its zenith in his new religion. Note, however, that
even at this stage of his thought, the Métis were not the sole beneficiaries of
Providence. They were the central actors in a plan of salvation which would

benefit all nations. They were a collective "suffering servant" who would take upon themselves the sins of all mankind.

Subsequent development in his thinking put increasing emphasis on the universal aspects of Riel's redemptive message. He did not abandon the special role of the Métis, but he began to take a greater interest in the fate of other peoples.

This change must have been connected with his interest in immigration. In 1878-79 he tried to associate himself with Bishop Ireland's Catholic Colonization Bureau, but the Bishop kept him at arm's length. Riel's initial impulse was to try to bring more French-Canadians to the West, as indeed he had tried to do in 1874-75; but gradually his horizon widened, perhaps from the example of Ireland's polyglot programme in Minnesota.

Unfortunately there is little written evidence about Riel's views on nationality in the period 1878-1884. One must make inferences from isolated and obscure texts, and scattered reports of conversations with him.

It is clear from two texts written in the summer of 1883, after Riel had paid a visit to Manitoba, that he still cherished the Métis identity. Both texts—a letter and a poem—have the same theme: the complementary strengths and weaknesses of the Métis, the French-Canadians, and the French. The Métis are physically the hardiest, and gifted with the simple virtues of a primitive people, but they can learn much from their more sophisticated cousins. There should be a gradual amalgamation of the three elements into one "nation Manitobaine/Des Métis-Canadiens-français".

> Métis et Canadiens ensemble
> Français, si nos trois éléments
> S'amalgament bien, il me semble
> Que nous serons un jour plus grands.[18]

The political side of this national sentiment was revealed in a conversation with a Montana sheriff. Riel disclosed a plan to found a Métis republic in Western Canada. He would gather the Métis from all over the American and Canadian West for this project. The government would be republican in form but theocratic in substance. Rome would be repudiated and the new religion installed.[19]

Wider dimensions of Riel's plan are suggested in two fragmentary and cryptic texts from this period. One speaks of "solving" the Indian question by universal miscegenation with white settlers of various nationalities.

> The tribes gathered in Manitoba would blend with the Métis and French-Canadians of that province. And the tribes in the North-West would mix with the Italians, Irish, Bavarians, Polish.
> Thus the entire native race of North America would make way to a new race: (French-Canadian Métis, Italian Métis, etc).[20]

These new nations would live under American protection and would learn from Washington how to govern themselves, "as the European nations have already learned from the Roman Empire how to obey and to command".[21]

The second text goes even farther. It seems to speak of a political and ecclesiastical reorganization of the entire New World. Riel's new religion would be established in an ecumenical form. His adherents drawn from the old Catholic Church would now be called "Episcopalian Catholics", "Lutheran Catholics", and so on. All these branches of the new religion, established in "all the nations of the New World", would be tied together through a complex system of councils in an "entente générale".[22]

Riel carried similar plans in his mind when he came to the Saskatchewan Valley in the summer of 1884. His initial approach to the Métis there was in the narrower terms of Métis nationalism. But his ecumenical vision had not vanished and would emerge into public view with the outbreak of the Rebellion.

Riel's first public pronouncements in the summer of 1884 were quite moderate, but behind the scenes he was beginning to spread his nationalism. On August 17 he had a blazing row with Father André. The priest was scandalized when Riel maintained that French-Canadians who moved to the North-West should merge into the Métis nationality, rather than the other way round. That month the Métis were expecting a visit from Sir Hector Langevin, federal Minister of Public Works. Riel planned to make a speech stressing the separate identity of the Métis, and comparing the patronizing attitude of the French-Canadians to that of the English.

Langevin cancelled his visit, but Riel found an even better occasion to publicize his views when Bishop Grandin visited Batoche in early September. At a great public meeeting, Riel asked Grandin to make St. Joseph the patron saint of the Métis, as St. John the Baptist was of the French-Canadians. The Métis national holiday would be July 24, one month after the feast day of John the Baptist. When Riel made the proposal, he advanced before the bishop, joining hands with a Frenchman and a French-Canadian to demonstrate the unity of all the children of France. Since July 24 had already passed for that year a special celebration was held on September 24.[23]

These events established in Riel's view the nationhood of the Métis. This was the foundation of later developments, as in February, 1885, when Riel publicly dedicated the Métis to the Sacred Heart and asked God to accept them as His favourite nation (*peuple de prédilection*).[24] It is no accident that the Rebellion was timed to break out on March 19, the feast of St. Joseph. The Métis were already assembled to celebrate the feast of their new patron saint when Riel announced that Rome had fallen, a new dispensation was in force, and a Provisional Government would be formed.

As events led up to the Rebellion, Riel began to reveal his larger designs. He promised the Métis on March 1 that he would bring "a countless multitude of nations" from the United States to help them.[25] A diary entry from about this time mentions the Italians, Poles, and other nations that Riel had in mind. "Thy Kingdom come", Riel wrote at the end of the passage, and starkly underlined the words.[26]

Riel's Provisional Government, the Exovedate, formally instituted the "Catholic, Apostolic, and Vital Church of the New World". Ignace Bourget was declared Pope, and Riel a prophet. The Sabbath was shifted from Sunday to Saturday. The Exovedes themselves became the Métis clergy which had never existed before.

Riel also spoke about his immigration scheme, but no one seems to have paid close attention. At least no one could later report it coherently. To get a good idea of it, one must go to his prison writings and to the explanation he gave at his trial.

Riel's leading idea was that the Métis had been promised one-seventh of the area of Manitoba through the land settlement which was provided in the Manitoba Act (see the next section). He felt that Canada had not fulfilled its share of this "treaty", so Manitoba and the North-West had reverted to the Métis. But they would not selfishly keep all for themselves. They would only retain their original proportion of one-seventh, which on the expanded scale of the entire North-West would amount to the entire province of Manitoba. This would be the homeland of the Métis, augmented by French and French-Canadian immigration. The rest of the country would also be divided into sevenths and given to different nationalities, who would mix with the Indians and develop new Métis races.

The details begin to blur at this point. Sometimes the immigrants are said to come directly from Europe, sometimes by way of the United States. The Belgians, Scandinavians, and Jews are usually given British Columbia to divide. The North-West Territories are usually allocated to the Italians, Irish, Bavarian and Poles; but on one occasion room is also made for Canada to have a seventh, and once also for the Anglo-Saxons. Finally northern Ontario is sometimes meted out to the Germans.[27]

Along with this national ecumenism, Riel also put forth a religious ecumenism. He spoke vaguely, even during the Rebellion, of reconciliation with Protestantism. He gave this theme considerable emphasis after his surrender. He added certain typical Protestant ideas, like personal interpretation of the Scriptures, to his doctrines; and he announced his readiness to accept Protestant ministers as validly ordained clergymen.[28] He spoke movingly at his trial:

> I wish to leave Rome aside, inasmuch as it is the cause of division between Catholics and Protestants...my children's children will shake hands with the Protestants of the new world in a friendly manner.[29]

Riel spent a good deal of effort during his imprisonment elaborating grandiose projects of political reform. In two letters to Sir. John A.Macdonald, he sketched the idea of an "Imperial Union" of Britain and the United States. Like Rome and Constantinople, London and Washington would be twin capitals of a multi-national empire. Small nations like the Métis, the Irish, and the French-Canadians would be secure within this vast structure. Riel himself might become Premier of Manitoba and renegotiate entry into Confederation. This would be a model to the Imperial Union of how to protect small nations. The Union would also undertake religious reform. A secretary of religion would be appointed to promote "the most perfect harmony possible among the different Christian denominations of (the) Colossal Dominion".[30]

Needless to say, the Prime Minister was not interested in Riel's plan. Riel then turned to President Grover Cleveland of the United States, sending him a petition which requested the annexation of Manitoba and the North-West.[31] Although this also brought no response, he did not lose confidence. Diary entries made in the month before his execution show him still considering both American annexation and the Imperial Union, singly or in combination. The constant factor was the Métis. No matter what course world politics might take, he foresaw a brilliant future for his people. "Manitoba will become totally French-Canadian Métis. Five hundred years from now, her Métis population will number forty million souls."[32]

By then the papacy would also be in Manitoba. Riel had outwardly made his peace with the Church, but he still cherished his project of religious reform. Now he tried to redraft it in orthodox terms. There would not be a break with Rome, but a dual papacy would be established. Leo XIII would continue to reign in the Old World, while Riel's old patron, Archbishop Taché, would become *Pontifex Major Totius Novi Mundi*. Both branches of the Universal Church would coexist in harmony.[33]

These shifting details of Riel's views on the Métis nation are confusing, bewildering, and may strike many readers as more than a little mad. The variation of ideas can be attributed as much to desperation as to Riel's exuberant imagination. Frustrated at every turn—sometimes by his own errors, sometimes by external circumstances—Riel sought to establish the Métis as a nation and protect their future in a multi-national structure. The intention itself is perfectly intelligible and worth recalling at a time when other groups within Canada—large like the Québécois and small like the Dene—are also asserting their nationhood.

Native Rights

Riel saw the Métis not only as a nation but as natives, like their English half-breed cousins. Through their descent from Indian ancestors, they shared aboriginal title to the land of British North America. They had both a moral and a legal right to compensation from the state in return for extinguishment of that title.

This general principle is not in question. It has always been recognized and acted upon by the British and Canadian state in dealings both with Indians and half-breeds. The practical question concerns the form which compensation will take. Here Riel's views are worth examining.

Let it be said immediately that Riel's true interest was in the Métis and to a lesser degree the English half-breeds. He had no real concern with the Indians. They were not involved in the first uprising at all. They played no role in Riel's thinking until late 1878, when he began to dream of unleashing the Plains Indians against Canada.[34] He made determined attempts to achieve a coalition of Indians in Montana over the winter of 1879-80 for that purpose. He was in touch with Sitting Bull, Crowfoot, and Big Bear; but these astute chiefs were cautious about Riel's advances, probably divining that the Indians were only grist for his mill. Remember that his long-range plan was to turn all Indians into Métis.

The Indian rising in the Rebellion of 1885 was inspired by the example of the Métis but was not a coordinated part of the same movement. Prior to the Rebellion, Riel had not tried to present himself to the Indians of Saskatchewan as their leader. In fact he had been rather reluctant to get too involved with them, fearing to alienate the white settlers. The petition sent to the federal cabinet on December 16, 1884, made only passing reference to the Indians, mentioning that they were "so reduced" that they had become a burden on the settlers who were compelled to relieve their indigence.[35] Riel only sought the active support of the Indians after the fighting had alredy begun. It was a tactical move, not a necessary consequence of his thinking. For all these reasons, the following discussion relates strictly to Riel's opinions about the aboriginal rights of the Métis.

The question of aboriginal rights played no role in the public debates of the first Rebellion. Riel's strategy was to present the Métis and half-breeds as civilized men, not savages. He emphasized their equality with the white settlers of Red River. All possessed the rights of British subjects. Riel demanded that Red River enter Confederation as a province, and that the local inhabitants possess the same rights as all Canadians. As part of this approach, he requested that the new province have control of public lands, as the older provinces did.[36]

If this demand had been granted, it would have allowed the new provincial government to deal with the land claims of the Métis. Riel probably intended this, but there is no documentation. In any event, the Prime Minister refused to give up control of public lands. He and Riel's emissary, Father Ritchot, finally reached a compromise, ratified in the Manitoba Act, according to which 1,400,000 acres would be set aside for distribution "among the children of the half-breed heads of families residing in the province" at the time of transfer to Canada.[37] Riel was apparently satisfied with this solution.

The land settlement was implemented in several phases. At first whole townships were to be set aside for the Métis and half-breeds. This approach was soon abandoned for a distribution of scrip redeemable for public lands anywhere in the province. "Heads of families", i.e. married half-breeds or Métis, received scrip for 160 acres; "children", i.e. unmarried Métis or half-breeds over eighteen years old, received scrip for 240 acres. The scrip could either serve as a location ticket or be sold on the open market for cash.

In one sense, this settlement was generous. Even more the 1,400,000 acres were ultimately granted. The Métis and half-breeds received for free enough property to set themselves up as farmers. But many were not able to make proper use of this opportunity. Some chose poor land, suitable for firewood and pasture, but not for farming. Many sold their scrip for a fraction of its worth and retreated to the west.[38]

Riel seems to have concluded from this sad experience that the Métis were not ready to enjoy all the rights of property ownership on a footing of perfect equality with white men. Thereafter his thinking moved to a more corporate conception of aboriginal rights.

An illustration is furnished by his attempt to obtain a reservation for the Métis in Montana in 1880. (This was not quite an instance of aboriginal rights, since the Métis, as British subjects, had no legal or moral claim on the American government; but in other respects it was analogous.) Riel composed a petition which said:

> We ask the Government to set apart a portion of land as a special reservation in this Territory, for the Half-breeds, as, scattered amongst other settlers, it becomes a very difficult matter for us to make a living, and owing to our present limited means, and want of experience in economy, we cannot compete with the majority of our fellow countrymen.[39]

The land, though granted collectively to the Métis, would be held in severalty. The petition also asked that a sum of money be appropriated to build schools and pay teachers, as well as to purchase agricultural implements, seed, and livestock. With that initial assistance, said Riel, the Métis would not need annual rations and provisions like the Indians. The Métis would also exclude liquor of all kinds from the reservation.

When the Métis invited Riel to the Saskatchewan country in 1884, they were chiefly concerned about the individual, not collective rights. Their major grievances were that they were having difficulty getting patents for lots on which they had squatted, and that there had not been in the North-West Territories an issue of scrip similar to that in Manitoba. Riel became the Métis advocate on these and certain related issues, but he also tried to inject into the debate much more sweeping proposals based implicitly on a theory of collective aboriginal rights.

His views may be found in a memorandum he wrote for Bishop Grandin in September, 1884. It called *inter alia* for issue of patents and of scrip, but also for steps which the local Métis had never thought of. The Government should sell 2,000,000 acres of public lands and deposit the proceeds to form an endowment fund for the Métis. The interest would be used to build schools, hospitals, and orphanages, and to assist Métis agriculture. Also, a hundred townships of land in the North-West, now swampy but potentially cultivable, should be set aside for distribution to future generations of Métis. And additional land should be set aside for the Métis of Manitoba because that province had been enlarged since 1870.[40]

Although Riel nowhere systematically elaborated the underlying rationale of these demands, it may be pieced together from scattered sources. He now regarded the Métis as having a collective right as a people to the territory of the entire North-West. The Manitoba Act, which in Riel's eyes had been a treaty between sovereign states, had established the precedent that the Métis title should be extinguished by a grant of one-seventh of the total land area (1,400,000 of the then 9,500,00 acres of Manitoba). This obligation had never been met in the North-West or the area added to Manitoba in 1881. Since this amount of land was far more than could sensibly be granted to the living Métis, part of it should be reserved to future generations, and part capitalized to form the Métis endowment fund. The details might be negotiable but in no case could the aboriginal title be extinguished by a simple, once-for-all grant of scrip to individual Métis, as had been done pursuant to the Manitoba Act.[41]

These ideas were dear to Riel, but they went beyond the spontaneous desires of the average Métis. They were also too radical for the white population of the district, with whom the Métis were pledged to prepare a joint petition. When the document was finally sent to Ottawa on December 16, 1884, it contained only the long-standing Métis demands for scrip and patents. Riel's wider demands were not mentioned.[42]

They also played no direct role in the subsequent Rebellion, except as one of several motives which impelled Riel to unconstitutional action. After his defeat, he tried to explain his views on the Métis aboriginal rights, both at his trial and in letters to important people, but without success.

For years afterwards the Dominion government continued to issue scrip to half-breeds to enable them to obtain individual lands. There have also been experiments with forms of common property, like St. Paul-des-Métis or the Métis reservations in northern Alberta. However, there has never been a settlement of Métis claims on the scale envisioned by Riel.

A century later, the details of his schemes have ceased to matter. But the principles which he espoused, no matter how confusedly, are worth remembering. These were: That the Métis had a collective aboriginal title to land which could not be extinguished by individual freehold grants. That provision must be made for future generations. That the Métis, in their present state of development, could not make full use of private property and hence had to be protected through some form of communal ownership. That the Métis would need education and financial assistance to make the transition from a nomadic to an agricultural existence.

Note also that Riel was confident about the capacity of the Métis to adapt to white civilization. He expected his people to settle down, learn to farm, and eventually become a leading force in North America. He in no way rejected Western civilization; he was looking for a method by which his people could participate in it while retaining their particular identity. He was quite different from some of our contemporaries who have come to doubt that white civilization has any value to native peoples.

Theocracy and Liberalism

Because circumstances made Riel an antagonist of the Canadian state, he has passed into left-wing folklore.[43] Many today see him as a champion of the oppressed, a defender of liberty, and so on. One political scientist recently told me he thought that Riel was really an anarchist. The truth is somewhat different.

Riel was given a strict and traditional education by the Sulpician Fathers, who were conservative philosophically and Conservative politically. Riel adopted both orientations. The Declaration of December 8, 1869, on which he collaborated with Father Dugas, is a most conservative document. As I have shown elsewhere, it is derived from J.-B. Du Voisin, a French royalist author, and through him from William Barclay, a sixteenth-century advocate of the divine right of kings.[44]

Thus it is not surprising that Riel accepted in 1874 the principles of the most conservative faction in Canadian politics, the ultramontanes of Quebec. Their leading ideas were absolute loyalty to an infallible pope, subordination of state to Church, and active clerical intervention in politics. Riel regarded Ignace Bourget, the leading ultramontane, as a saint. Bourget's views are epitomized in his famous exhortation: "Let each say in his heart, 'I hear my *curé*, my *curé* hears the bishop, the bishop hears the Pope, and the Pope hears our Lord Jesus Christ".[45] Riel idolized, in addition to Bourget, the reigning pontiff Pius IX, whose *Syllabus of Errors* had condemned liberalism in 1854. Pius often made important public gestures on December 8, the feast of the Immaculate Conception; and Riel imitated this to the extent that his mission as "Prophet of the New World" also began on December 8, 1875.

The enemies of the ultramontanes were liberals philosophically and Liberals politically. Riel, in his period of religious exaltation (1875-78), used "liberalism" as a synonym for evil. He defined it as "turning one's back on God, to flee the duties of lasting virtue for the love of ease, of self-indulgence, and of sensual pleasure".[46] Liberalism was a kind of world-conspiracy of evil. Anyone opposed to Riel or the Pope was a liberal: those who were keeping Riel in the asylum, Sir John A. Macdonald, Bismarck. Ironically even Pius IX became a liberal in Riel's mind when the latter broke with the Church. Riel's hyper-ultramontanism in this period surely made him "more Catholic than the Pope", as the old saying goes.

Riel also adopted and exaggerated ultramontane preferences in European politics. His writings of this period contain sympathetic references to "Henry V", the Bourbon pretender to the French throne, and to Don Carlos, his Spanish counterpart. Riel saw himself as being in much the same situation as this reactionary pair. Like them, he was a divinely annointed ruler, prevented by the forces of "liberalism" from assuming his rightful position.[47]

His positive notion of political order became correspondingly extreme. Where the Quebec ultramontanes had preached subordination of state to Church, Riel called for fusion of the two in a theocracy. He would be both priest and king, like David of old. Society would become a kingdom of saints ruled by ministers of the new religion.

> For eighteen hundred years, the true priesthood has had, properly speaking, nothing but means of persuasion to convert the world . . . (But now) Jesus Christ wants to perfect the government of His Church and to make His apostles able to exercise charitable coercion on men . . .[48]

"Charitable coercion" would establish the "Catholic, Apostolic and Vital Church of the Shining Mountains" as the only accepted religion in a reformed society.

This theocratic tone became somewhat more moderate in Riel's later life, as his views grew more ecumenical. One will not find in his post-1878 writings the same badly stated determination to fuse church and state and establish the new dispensation by force. Such a policy would have been incompatible with attracting the support of different denominations and nationalities, as Riel hoped to do.

But the underlying impulse was probably still theocratic. Certainly Riel's choice of political heroes remained the same to the end of his life. In prison, he wanted to rename the North Pole after Gabriel Garcia Moreno, dictator of Ecuador, 1861-75.[49] His regime was semi-theocratic, and he had officially dedicated the entire country to the protection of the Sacred Heart of Jesus. Riel also thought that he himself might be the successor to "Henry V", who had died in 1883. Riel wrote:

> What the world expected in the person of Henry V is now found in the Prophet of the New World, Louis "David" Riel, who through his mother Julie de la Gimodière is one of the princes descended from Louis XI.[50]

This sentence is part of a fantastic daydream written in prison, in which Riel imagines himself as head of state in France. He will unite behind himself the hostile factions of Republicans, Monarchists, and Bonapartists. He will rule for life like a king, subject to a plebiscite every seven years like Louis

Napoleon. His demeanour will be unassuming, like that of a good republican president; and his only title will be "Exovede" (as in the North-West Rebellion). A time of universal harmony will ensue; and all Frenchmen will enjoy liberty, equality, and fraternity, while the rights of the true Church will be reestablished.

It is obvious that while Riel was now more tolerant and inclusive than he had been at an earlier stage, his thinking was still visionary and utopian. His goal was, as ever, something like a kingdom of saints living under divine supervision. It was still basically a theocracy, albeit more relaxed.

This is not suprising. Riel was concerned with freedom chiefly in the sense of group autonomy. As a moral reformer, he disliked the individual liberty of a free society. He had the soul of Savonarola and Calvin, not of Locke and Jefferson.

Appendix

Louis Riel: A Preliminary Bibliography 1963 - 1968

Thérèse E. Lafontaine

As the title indicates, this compilation of scholarly publications on Riel and the Rebellions is very limited in scope. All works published on Riel prior to 1963 are excluded. The year 1963 was chosen to begin the bibliography for an excellent reason: it is the year of the publication of George F. G. Stanley's definitive text *Louis Riel* (Toronto: Ryerson, 1963). Whereas the date 1963 is rigorously precise as a demarcation point, we should recognize that the date 1978 is tenuous and indefinite. Many books and periodicals recently issued or theses just completed have not yet been catalogued or indexed. A few 1979 entries have been enclosed.

In this preliminary bibliography, I have attempted to select all books, pamphlets, essays in collections, articles in learned journals and theses concerned in whole or in part with Riel. I have included new editions of older texts, for example, the second edition of Lewis H. Thomas' *The Struggle for Responsible Government in the North-West Territories* 1870-1897 (Toronto: Univ. of Toronto Press, 1978) (first edition 1956). I have also found it worthwhile to note reprints and facsimile editions of Western Canadiana. However, government documents, review articles and newspaper reports have not been incorporated in the bibliography.

The bibliographical format presents in an orderly and clear manner the various items compiled. The material is arranged according to the following eight divisions:

     I. Bibliographies
    II. Specific Books and Pamphlets
   III. Articles
   IV. Articles in Collected Essays
    V. General Books and Pamphlets
   VI. Theses
  VII. Facsimile Editions
VIII. Literary Texts

Only the reference sources which proved to be especially useful in making the bibliography are listed in the first section. You will find all books and pamphlets pertaining directly to Riel in the category "Specific Books and Pamphlets". Each essay or research paper in a collection is entered separately under the heading "Articles in Collected Essays". In the category "General Books and Pamphlets", whenever possible, I have tried to indicate the exact chapter relating to Riel or the North-West.

Our objective has been to establish an accurate and a fairly comprehensive bibliography. The researcher will discover that the merit of the present bibliography lies primarily in its accuracy rather than in its exhaustiveness since only the publications which have been verified personally are included. All bibliographical information was examined except, of course, theses which could not be consulted. If mistakes have inadvertently been made during the process of selection and collocation, I take full responsibility. Throughout the bibliography, I have adhered to the specifications of the *MLA Handbook* (1977). Page numbers have been inserted in order to distinguish books from pamphlets.

For various reasons, 39 items, particularly in the areas of recent articles, general books and literary texts, have not been located and verified; therefore this data does not appear in the bibliography. For example, an article like Gilles Martel's "Les Indiens dans la pensée messianique de Louis Riel," *Recherches Amérindiennes au Québec,* 8 (1978), 123-137, a novel like R. D. Symonds, *Still the Wind Blows; a historical novel of the Canadian Northwest, 1860-1916* (Saskatoon: Western Producer Prairie Books, 1971), or a facsimile edition like T. A. Haultain, *A History of Riel's Second Rebellion and How it was Quelled* (North Vancouver: C. G. Bainbridge, 1976) remain unexamined. I look forward to the presentation of publications like these in a forthcoming supplement.

Bibliographies

Abler, Thomas S., and Sally M. Weaver. *A Canadian Indian Bibliography 1960 - 1970*. Toronto: University of Toronto Press, 1974, pp. 664 - 674.

Arora, Ved Parkash. *Louis Riel: A Bibliography*. Regina: Provincial Library, 1972. 66pp. (Bibliographic Services)

————. *Louis Riel: A Selected Bibliography*. Regina: Provincial Library, 1973. 32pp. (Bibliographic Services Division)

Artibise, Alan F. J. *Western Canada Since 1870: A Select Bibliography and Guide*. Vancouver: University of British Columbia, 1978. 312 pp.

Beaulieu, André, Jean Hamelin et Benoît Bernier. *Guide d'histoire du Canada*. Québec: Presses de l'Université, Laval, 1969. 540 pp. (Cahiers de l'Institut d'histoire No. 13)

"Bibliographie d'histoire de l'Amérique française — (Publications récentes)." *Revue d'histoire de l'Amérique française,* 21, No. 1 (juin 1967), 160 -174. ---(a compilation found in every issue thereafter)

Bowsfield, Hartwell. "The West." *Canada Since 1867: A Bibliographic Guide*. Eds. J. L. Granatstein and Paul Stevens. Toronto: Hakkert, 1974, pp. 87 - 107.

————. "The West: History and Politics." *Read Canadian: A Book About Canadian Books*. Eds. Robert Fulford, David Godfrey and Abraham Rotstein. Toronto: James Lewis and Samuel, 1972, pp. 20 - 29.

Canadian Books in Print, 1977: Subject Index. Ed. Martha Pluscauskas. Toronto: University of Toronto Press, 1978. 680 pp.

Canadian Index to Periodicals and Documentary Films: An Author and Subject Index. Vol. 16 (1963), --- (A continuing serial published by the Canadian Library Association)

Canadian Selection: Books and Periodicals for Libraries. Comps. Edith Jarvi, Isabel McLean and Catharine MacKenzie. Toronto: University of Toronto Press, 1978. 1060pp. (Centre for Research in Librarianship)

Canadian Theses. Ottawa: National Library of Canada, 1965 -- (a compilation for the years 1963 - 1964 to 1971-1972)

Canadiana. Publications of Canadian Interest Received by the National Library. Ottawa: National Library of Canada 1963 --- (an annual publication)

Catalogue of the Glenbow Historical Library, The Glenbow-Alberta Institute Library. 4 vols. Calgary, Alberta: Boston, Mass.: G. K. Hall, 1973.

Dhand, L., L. Hunt and L. Goshawk. *Louis Riel: An Annotated Bibliography.* Saskatoon: University of Saskatchewan, 1972. 41pp. (Research Resources Centre, College of Education)

Dictionary of Canadian Biography, 1871 - 1880. Vol. 10. Toronto/Québec: University of Toronto Press and Presses de l'Université Laval, 1972. 894pp.

Dorge, Lionel. *Introduction à l'étude des Franco-Manitobains: Essai historique et bibliographique.* Saint-Boniface: La Société Historique de Saint-Boniface, 1973. 298 pp.

Fancy, Margaret. *A Bibliography of the Works of George Francis Gillman Stanley.* Sackville: Ralph Pickard Bell Library, Mount Allison University, 1976. 52pp. (Bibliography Series No. 1)

Fox, Rosalea. "Bibliography." In *Strange Empire: Louis Riel and the Métis People.* Joseph K. Howard. Toronto: James, Lewis and Samuel, 1974, pp. 567-588.

Harvard University Library. Widener Library Shelflist, 20 Canadian History and Literature. Cambridge, Mass.: Harvard University Press, 1968. 411 pp.

Jain, Sushil Kumar. *Louis 'David' Riel and the North-West Rebellion: A List of References.* Regina: University of Saskatchewan, 1965. 19 pp. (Regina Campus Library)

Klinck, Carl F. and Reginald E. Watters. "Bibliography." *Canadian Anthology.* 3rd ed. Toronto: Gage Educational Publishing, 1974, pp. 646-721.

Koester, C.B. *A Bibliography of Selected Theses in the Library of the Univer-*

sity of Alberta (Edmonton) Relating to Western Canada, 1915 - 1965. Edmonton: Western Canada Research Project, 1965. 21 pp.

Lochhead, Douglas. *Bibliography of Canadian Bibliographies.* 2nd ed. Toronto: University of Toronto Press, 1972. 312pp. (Bibliographical Society of Canada)

McLeod, Gordon Duncan. *A Descriptive Bibliography of the Candian Prairie Novel, 1871 - 1970.* Ph.D. Thesis. Winnipeg: University of Manitoba, 1974. 253 pp. (a photocopy of the typescript)

Peel, Bruce Braden. *A Bibliography of the Prairie Provinces to 1953 With Biographical Index.* 2nd ed. Toronto: University of Toronto Press, 1973. 780 pp.

"Recent Publications Relating to Canada." *Canadian Historical Review,* 44 (1963), 82- 87. --- (bibliography found in every issue)

Regehr, T.D. "Historiography of the Canadian Plains After 1870." In *A Region of the Mind: Interpreting The Western Canadian Plains.* Ed. Richard Allen. Regina: University of Saskatchewan, 1973, pp. 87 - 101. (Canadian Plains Studies Centre)

Register of Post-Graduate Dissertations in Progress in History and Related Subjects. Vol. 1 (1966) --- (Comp. Public Archives of Canada and Publ. Canadian Historical Association)

Répertoire des historiens du Québec et du Canada français. 3ième ed. Québec: L'Université du Québec, 1977. 186 pp. (Section québecoise du Comité international des historiens et géographes francophones)

Ryder, Dorothy E. *Canadian Reference Sources: A Selective Guide.* Ottawa: Canadian Library Association, 1973. 185 pp.

―――. *The Canadian West and the North: A Bibliographical Overview.* Edmonton: University of Alberta Library, 1978. 13 pp. (Publ. for the Bibliographical Society of Canada)

Scott, Michael M. *A Bibliography of Western Canadian Studies Relating to Manitoba.* Winnipeg: Western Canada Research Council, 1967. 79 pp.

Swainson, Donald. "It's the Riel Thing." *Books in Canada,* 8, No. 5 (May 1979), 14 - 15.

Thibault, Claude. *Bibliographia Canadiana*. Don Mills, Ontario: Longman Canada Limited, 1973. 795 pp.

Toye, William. *Supplement to the Oxford Companion to Canadian History and Literature*. Toronto: Oxford University Press, 1973. 318 pp.

Vaugeois, Denis. "Louis Riel, (huit études.)" *Revue d'histoire de l'Amérique française,* 30, No. 3 (déc. 1976), 428 - 431.

Ward, W. Peter. "Western Canada: Recent Historical Writing." *Queen's Quarterly,* 85, No. 2 (Summer 1978), 271 - 288.

Specific Books and Pamphlets

Anderson, Frank W. "1885"; *The Riel Rebellion.* Aldergrove, B.C.: Frontier Publishing, 1962. 80 pp. (Frontier Books No. 3)

————. *Riel's Manitoba Uprising.* Aldergrove, B.C.: Frontier Publishing, 1974. 64 pp. (Frontier Books No. 31)

Bowsfield, Hartwell. *Louis Riel: le patriote rebelle.* Trad. Pierre-Louis Gélinas. Montréal: Editions du Jour, 1973. 173 pp.

————. *Louis Riel: Rebel of the Western Frontier or Victim of Politics and Prejudice?* Toronto: The Copp Clark Publishing, 1969. 227 pp. (Issues in Canadian History).

Campbell, Maria. *Riel's People: How the Métis Lived.* Vancouver: Douglas and McIntyre, 1978. 47 pp.

Cerbelaud, Salagnac Georges. *La Révolte des Métis: Louis Riel héros ou rebelle.* (Tours): Mame, 1971. 210 pp.

Charlebois, Peter. *Chronology based on The Life of Louis Riel.* Toronto: N C Press, 1977. (New Canada Publications)

————. *The Life of Louis Riel.* Toronto: N C Press, 1975. 255 pp. (New Canada Publications)

Dorge, Lionel. *Louis Riel, Manitoban 1844 - 1885.* (Winnipeg): Manitoba Centennial Corporation, 1971. 11 pp.

Flanagan, Thomas, ed. *The Diaries of Louis Riel.* Edmonton: Hurtig Publishers, 1976. 187 pp.

————. *Louis 'David' Riel: Prophet of the New World.* Toronto: University of Toronto Press, 1979. 216 pp.

Howard, Joseph. *Strange Empire: Louis Riel and the Métis People.* New York: W. Morrow, 1952; rpt. Toronto: James, Lewis and Samuel, 1974. 601 pp.

Howard, Richard. *Riel.* Toronto: Clarke, Irwin and Company, n.d. (Jackdaw, no. c2)

Jordan, Mary. *To Louis from your sister who loves you - Sara Riel.* Toronto: Griffin House, 1974. 172 pp.

Lusty, Terrance W.J. *Louis Riel: Humanitarian.* Calgary: Métis Historical Society, 1973. 28 pp.

Martel, Gilles, Glen Campbell and Thomas Flanagan, eds. *Louis Riel: Poésies de jeunesse.* Saint-Boniface: Editions du Blé, 1977. 161 pp.

Mika, Nick and Helma Mika, comps. *The Riel Rebellion, 1885,* Belleville, Ontario: Mika Silk Screening, 1972. 355 pp. (reprints of newspaper reports of 1885).

Morton, Desmond. *The Last War Drum: the North West Campaign of 1885.* Toronto: Hakkert, 1972. 193 pp. (Canadian War Museum Historical Publications No. 5).

————, ed. *The Queen v Louis Riel.* Toronto: University of Toronto Press 1974. 383 pp. (Social History of Canada No. 19).

———— and Reginald H. Roy, eds. *Telegrams of the North-West Campaign, 1885.* Toronto: The Champlain Society, 1972. 431pp. (Publications of the Champlain Society No. 47.)

Neering, Rosemary. *Louis Riel.* Don Mills, Ontario: Fitzhenry and Whiteside, 1977. 63pp.

Oppen, William A. *The Riel Rebellions: A Cartographic History.* Toronto: University of Toronto Press, 1979. (Forthcoming)

Osler, Edmund Boyd. *Louis Riel, un homme à pendre.* Trad. Rossel Vien. Montréal: Editions du Jour, 1969. 295pp. (Collection l'Histoire vivante No. 2)

Pearl, Stanley. *Louis Riel: A Volatile Legacy.* Toronto: Maclean-Hunter, 1971. 64pp. (Canadian Issues)

Rumilly, Robert. *Histoire de la province de Québec.* Vol. 5: *Louis Riel.* Montréal: Editions Valiquette, 1941; rpt. Montréal: Fides, 1973. 313pp.

Silver, A. I. and Marie-France Valleur. *The North-West Rebellion.* Vancouver: The Copp Clark Publishing, 1967. 68pp. (Problems in Canadian History)

Stanley, George F. G. *Louis Riel.* Toronto: The Ryerson Press, 1963. 431pp.

―――. *Louis Riel.* Conférence donnée à la Société Historique de Saint-Boniface le 17 janvier 1970. 15pp.

―――. *Louis Riel: Patriot or Rebel?* Ottawa: Canadian Historical Association, 1970. 28pp. (Canadian Historical Association Booklets No. 2)

Woodcock, George. *Gabriel Dumont: The Métis Chief and his Lost World.* Edmonton: Hurtig Publishers, 1976. 256 pp.

Articles

Allan, Iris, ed. "A Riel Rebellion Diary." *Alberta Historical Review,* 12, No. 3 (Summer 1964), 15 - 25. (diary of Robert K. Allan, March 26th to July 13th 1885)

Allen, R.S. "Big Bear." *Saskatchewan History,* 25, No. 1 (Winter 1972), 1 -17.

Baptie, Sue. "Edgar Dewdney." *Alberta Historical Review,* 16, No. 4 (Autumn 1968), 1 - 10.

Bartlett, Fred E. "The Fall of Fort Garry." *The Beaver,* 296 (Spring 1966), 48 - 52.

————. "The Ordeal of William Mactavish." *The Beaver,* 295 (Autumn 1964), 42 - 47.

Bingaman, Sandra Estlin. "The Trials of Poundmaker and Big Bear, 1885." *Saskatchewan History,* 28, No. 3 (Autumn 1975), 81 - 94.

————. "The Trials of the 'White Rebels', 1885." *Saskatchewan History,* 25, No. 2 (Spring 1972), 41 - 54.

Boissonnault, Charles-Marie. "L'Expédition du nord-ouest: le Rapport Wolseley." *Proceedings of the Royal Society of Canada,* 4th series, 8 (1970), 123 - 131.

Bowsfield, Hartwell, ed. "Louis Riel's Letter to President Grant, 1875." *Saskatchewan History,* 21, No. 2 (Spring 1968), 67 - 75.

Breen, David H. "'Timber Tom' and the North-West Rebellion." *Alberta Historical Review,* 19, No. 3 (Summer 1971), 1 - 7.

Brown, Desmond H. "The Meaning of Treason in 1885." *Saskatchewan History,* 28, No. 2 (Spring 1975), 65 - 73.

Cherwinski, W.J.C. "Honoré Joseph Jaxon, Agitator, Disturber, producer of plans to make men think, and Chronic Objector..." *Canadian Historical Review,* 46, No. 2 (June 1965), 122 - 133.

Cubb, Sally, "Red River Exodus." *Arbos,* 1, No. 3 (January 1965), 17 - 28.

Creighton, Donald. "John A. Macdonald, Confederation and the Canadian West." *Historical and Scientific Society of Manitoba Transactions,* Series 3, 23 (1966 - 1967), 5 - 13. Rpt. in *Minorities, Schools, and Politics.* Eds. Ramsay Cook, Craig Brown and Carl Berger. Toronto: University of Toronto Press, 1969, pp. 1 - 9. Rpt in *Historical Essays on the Prairie Provinces.* Ed. Donald Swainson. Toronto: McClelland and Stewart, 1970, pp. 60 - 70.

Denny, C.D., "In Memory of Mary Rose (Pritchard) Sayers, The Last Witness. *Saskatchewan History,"* 24, No. 2 (Spring 1971), 63 - 72 (Frog Lake, 1885).

Desjardins, Edouard et Charles Dumas. "Le Complexe médical de Louis Riel." *L'Union médicale du Canada,* 99, No. 9 (Sept. 1970), 1656 -1661; 99, No. 10 (Oct. 1970), 1870 - 1878.

Dorge, Lionel. "Bishop Taché and the Confederation of Manitoba, (1869 - 1870)" *Historical and Scientific Society of Manitoba Transactions, Series 3, 26 (1969 - 1970), 93 - 110.*

———. "The Métis and Canadian Councillors of Assiniboia." *The Beaver,* 305 (Summer 1974), 12 - 19; 305 (Autumn 1974), 39 - 45; 305 (Winter 1974), 51 - 58.

Fergusson, Charles Bruce, ed. "A Glimpse of 1885." *Saskatchewan History,* 21, No. 1 (Winter 1968), 24 - 29. (Reminiscences of Harold E. Ross).

Fisher, S.T. ed., "An Episode of the North-West Rebellion, 1885." *Saskatchewan History,* 20, No. 2 (Spring 1967), 71 - 75. (Recollections of G.J. Kinnaird).

Flanagan, Thomas E. "Louis 'David' Riel: Prophet, Priest-King, Infallible Pontiff." *Journal of Canadian Studies, 9, No. 3 (August 1974), 15 - 25.*

———. "Louis Riel: A Case Study in Involuntary Psychiatric Confinement." *Canadian Psychiatric Association Journal,* 23, No. 7 (Nov. 1978), 463 -468.

———. "Louis Riel's Religious Beliefs: A Letter to Bishop Taché." *Saskatchewan History,* 27, No. 1 (Winter 1974), 15 - 28.

Flanagan, Thomas E. "The Mission of Louis Riel." *Alberta History,* 23, No. 1 (Winter 1975), 1 - 12.

――――. "Political Theory of the Red River Resistance: The Declaration of December 8, 1869." *Canadian Journal of Political Science,* 11, No. 1 (March 1978), 153 - 164.

―――― "The Religion of Louis Riel." *The Quarterly of Canadian Studies for Secondary School,* 4, No. 1 (1975), 3 - 14.

――――. "The Riel 'Lunacy Commission' The Report of Dr. Valade." *Revue de l'Université d'Ottawa,* 46, No. 1 (janv. - mars 1976), 108 - 127.

Foster, John E. "Missionaries, Mixed-Bloods and the Fur Trade: Four Letters of the Rev. William Cockran, Red River Settlement, 1830 - 1833." *The Western Canadian Journal of Anthropology,* 3, No. 1 (1972), 94 - 125.

Fraser, W. B. "Big Bear, Indian Patriot." *Alberta Historical Review,* 14, No. 2 (Spring 1966), 1 -13. Rpt. in *Historical Essays on the Prairie Provinces.* Ed. Donald Swainson. Toronto: McClelland and Steward, 1970, pp. 71 -88.

Greenland, Cyril. "The Life and Death of Louis Riel: (A Study in Forensic Psychiatry) - Part 11 - Surrender, Trial, Appeal and Execution." *Canadian Psychiatric Association Journal,* 10, No. 4 (Aug. 1965), 253 - 259.

――――, and John D. Griffin. "William Henry Jackson (1861 - 1952): Riel's Secretary: Another Case of Involuntary Commitment." *Canadian Psychiatric Association Journal,* 23, No. 7 (Nov 1978), 469 - 477.

Hafter, Ruth. "The Riel Rebellion and Manifest Destiny." *Dalhousie Review.* 45 (1965 - 1966), 447 - 456.

Hall, D. J. "The Half-Breed Claims Commission." *Alberta History,* 25, No. 2 (Spring 1977), 1 - 8.

Harrington, Lyn. "Prairie Battlefield." *Canadian Geographical Journal,* 66, No. 1 (Jan. 1963), 28 - 37.

Hicks, Joseph. "With Hatton's Scouts in Pursuit of Big Bear." *Alberta Historical Review,* 18, No. 3 (Summer 1970), 14 - 23.

Irvine, A. G. Col. "A Parley with Big Bear." *Alberta Historical Review,* 11,

No. 4 (1963), 19, (article originally appeared in the *Lethbridge Herald,* Jan. 7, 1909)

Kennedy, Howard Angus. "Memories of '85." *Canadian Geographical Journal,* 70, No. 5 (May 1965), 154 - 161.

Lalonde, André N. "Colonization Companies in the 1880's." *Saskatchewan History,* 24, No. 3 (Autumn 1971), 101 - 114.

———. "The North-West Rebellion and Its Effects on Settlers and Settlement in the Canadian West." *Saskatchewan History,* 27, No. 3 (Autumn 1974), 95 -102.

Landon, Fred, ed. "Recollections of the North West Rebellion of 1885: Laurids Hyttenrauch." *Western Ontario Historical Notes,* 20, No. 1 (1964), 29 - 36

Larmour, Jean. "Edgar Dewdney and the Aftermath of the Rebellion." *Saskatchewan History,* 23, No. 3 (Autumn 1970), 105 - 117.

Littmann, S.K. "A Pathography of Louis Riel." *Canadian Psychiatric Association Journal,* 23, No. 7 (Nov. 1978), 449 - 462.

McArthur, Peter. "The Red River Rebellion." *Manitoba Pageant,* 17, No. 2 (Winter 1972), 16 - 18; 18, No. 3 (Spring 1973), 22 - 24. (recollections recorded in 1934 and 1935)

MacDonald, R. H. "Fort Battleford, Saskatchewan." *Canadian Geographical Journal,* 67, No. 2 (August 1963), 54 - 61.

McLean, W.J. "Tragic Events at Frog Lake and Fort Pitt during the North West Rebellion." *Manitoba Pageant,* 17, No. 2 (Winter 1972), 2 - 9; 17, No. 3 (Spring 1972), 19 - 24; 18, No. 1 (Autumn 1972), 22 - 24; 18, No. 2 (Winter 1973), 4 - 8; 18, No. 3 (Spring 1973), 11 - 16.

Mallory, Enid Swerdfeger. "The Life of Lower Fort Garry." *Canadian Geographical Journal,* 66, No. 4 (April 1963), 116 - 123.

Markson, E.R. "The Life and Death of Louis Riel: (A Study in Forensic Psychiatry) Part 1 - A Psychoanalytic Commentary." *Canadian Psychiatric Association Journal,* 10, No. 4 (Aug. 1965), 244 - 252.

Martel, Gilles. "Louis Riel: ferveur nationaliste et foi religieuse." *Relations,* 37, No. 425 (avril 1977), 103 - 105.

Miller, Carman, ed. "Lord Melgund and the North-West Campaign of 1885." *Saskatchewan History,* 22, No. 3 (Autumn 1969), 81 - 108.

Mitchner, Alyn E. "William Pearce and Federal Government Activity in the West, 1874 - 1904." *Canadian Public Administration,* 10, No. 2 (June 1967), 235 -243.

Morton, Desmond. "Cavalry or Police: Keeping the Peace on Two Adjacent Frontiers, 1870 -1900." *Journal of Canadian Studies,* 12, No. 2 (Spring 1977), 24 - 37.

————. "Des Canadiens errants: French Canadian Troops in the North-West Campaign of 1885." *Journal of Canadian Studies,* 5, No. 3 (August 1970), 28 - 39.

Morton, W. L. "The 1870 Outfit at Red River." *The Beaver,* 300 (Spring 1970), 4 - 11.

————. "Manitoba's Historic Role." *Historical and Scientific Society of Manitoba Transactions,* Series 3, 19 (1962 - 1963), 50 - 57.

————. "Two Young Men, 1869: Charles Mair and Louis Riel." *Historical and Scientific Society of Manitoba Transactions,* Series 3, 30 (1973 -1974), 33 - 43.

O'Brodovich, Lloyd. "Plains Cree Acculturation in the Nineteenth Century: A Study of Injustice." Na' Pao: *Saskatchewan Anthropology Journal,* 2, No. 1 (1969), 2 - 23.

Painchaud, Robert. "Les Origines des peuplements de langue française dans l'Ouest canadien, 1870 - 1920: mythes et réalités." *Mémoires de la Société Royale du Canada, 4ième série,* 13 (1975), 109 - 121.

Pannekoek, Fritz. "Protestant Agricultural Zions for the Western Indian." *Journal of the Canadian Church Historical Society,* 14, No. 3 (Sept. 1972), 55 - 66.

————. "The Rev. Griffiths Owen Corbett and the Red River Civil War of 1869 - 1870." *Canadian Historical Review,* 57, No. 2 (June 1976), 133 -149.

Pearce, William. "Causes of the Riel Rebellion: A Personal View." *Alberta Historical Review,* 16, No. 4 (Autumn 1968), 19 - 26. (an address given to the Alberta Land Surveyor's Association in 1921)

Pennefather, John P. "A Surgeon with the Alberta Field Force." *Alberta History,* 26, No. 4 (Autumn 1978), 1 - 14. (excerpt from the pamphlet entitled *Thirteen Years on the Prairies,* 1892)

Riel, Louis. "Les dernières paroles de Riel." Trad. par Jacques Godbout. *Liberté,* 8, No. 1 (janv - fév. 1966), 20 - 27. (une adaptation libre du discours de Riel par John Colombo)

————. "Du Dieu du ciel la Providence...." *Mosaic,* 3, No. 3 (Spring 1970), 123 - 126.

————. "Journal de prison." *Ecrits du Canada français,* 13 (1962), 305 -353.

————. "Lettre de Louis Riel à sa femme. (5 octobre 1885)" *Bulletin des recherches historiques,* 69, No. 4 (oct. 1967), 160.

————. "To Sir John A. MacDonald." Trans. John Glassco. *Canadian Literature,* 37 (Summer 1968), 40 - 45. Rpt. in *The Poetry of French Canada in Translation.* Ed. John Glassco. Toronto: Oxford University Press, 1970, pp. 28 - 34.

Roberts, A.C. "The Surveys in the Red River Settlement in 1869." *The Canadian Surveyor,* 24, No. 2 (June 1970), 238-248.

Rowand, Evelyn. "The Rebellion at Lac La Biche." *Alberta Historical Review,* 21, No. 3 (Summer 1973), 1-9.

Roy, R.H. "Rifleman Forin in the Riel Rebellion." *Saskatchewan History,* 21, No. 3 (Autumn 1968), 100 - 111.

Ryerson, Stanley. "Riel vs Anglo-Canadian Imperialism." *Canadian Dimension,* 7, Nos. 1-2 (June-July 1970), M7-M8.

Shrive, Norman. "Poets and Patriotism: Charles Mair and Tecumseh." *Canadian Literature,* 20, (Spring 1964), 15-26.

————. "Poet and Politics: Charles Mair at Red River". *Canadian Literature,* 17, (Summer 1963), 6 - 21.

Silver, A.I. "French Canada and the Prairie Frontier, 1870-1890." *Canadian Historical Review,* 50, No. 1 (March 1969), 11-36.

Sprenger, G. Herman. "The Métis Nation: Buffalo Hunting vs Agriculture in the Red River Settlement (circa 1810-1870)." *The Western Canadian Journal of Anthropology,* 3, No. 1 (1972), 158-178.

Stanley, George F.G. "Indian Raid at Lac la Briche." *Alberta History,* 24, No. 3 (Summer 1976), 25-27.

————. "L'Invasion fénienne au Manitoba: Un journal contemporain." *Revue d'histoire de l'Amérique française,* 17, No. 2, (sept. 1963), 258-268.

————. ed. "le Journal de l'Abbé N.-J. Ritchot—1870." *Revue de l'histoire de l'Amerique française,* 17, No. 4 (mars 1964), 537 - 564.

————. "Louis Riel". *Revue de l'histoire de l'Amérique française,* 18, No. 1 (juin 1964) 14 - 26. (causerie prononcée le, 25 avril 1964).

Thomas, Lewis H., ed. "Louis Riel's Petition of Rights, 1884." *Saskatchewan History,* 23, No. 1 (Winter 1970), 16-26.

Toupin, Robert S.J. "Faillait—il exécuter Louis Riel?" *Revue de l'Université Laurentienne,* 1, No. 2 (nov. 1968), 49 - 60.

Turner, R.E. "The Life and Death of Louis Riel: (A Study in Forensic Psychiatry) - Part III - Medico-Legal Issues." *Canadian Psychiatric Association Journal,* 10, No. 4, (August 1965), 256-263.

Vien, Rossel. "La Correspondance de Sara Riel." *Ecrits du Canada français,* 22 (1966), 243-276.

Williams, Milton. "Twice Disappointed." *Alberta Historical Review,* 11, No. 4 (Autumn 1963), 15-18. (The Steele Scouts during the North-West Rebellion).

Woolworth, Nancy L. "Gingras, St. Joseph and the Métis in the Northern Red River Valley: 1843-1873." *North Dakota History,* 42, No. 4 (Fall 1975), 16-27.

Articles in Collected Essays

Flanagan, Thomas E. "Catastrophe and the Millennium: A New View of Louis Riel." *Canadian Plains Studies 3: Religion and Society in the Prairie West.* Ed. Richard Allen. Regina: Canadian Plains Research Center, 1974, pp. 35-51.

———. "Louis Riel: Insanity and Prophecy," *The Settlement of the West.* Ed. Howard Palmer. Calgary: University of Calgary Comprint Publishing Company, 1977, pp. 15 - 36.

Foster, John E. "The Origins of the Mixed Bloods in the Canadian West." *Essays on Western History, in Honour of Lewis Gwynne Thomas.* Ed. Lewis H. Thomas. Edmonton: University of Alberta Press, 1976, pp. 71 - 80.

———. "Rupert's Land and the Red River Settlement, 1820 - 1870." *The Prairie West to 1905: A Canadian Sourcebook.* Ed Lewis G. Thomas. Toronto: Oxford University Press, 1975, pp. 19 - 69.

Huel, Raymond J. "French-Speaking Bishops and the Cultural Mosaic in Western Canada." *Canadian Plains Studies 3: Religion and Society in the Prairie West.* Ed. Richard Allen. Regina: Canadian Plains Research Center, 1974, pp. 53 - 64.

Knox, Olive. "The Question of Louis Riel's Insanity." *The Other Natives, the - les Métis,* 1700-1885. Vol. 1. Eds. Antoine S. Lussier and D. Bruce Sealey. Winnipeg: Manitoba Métis Federation Press and Editions Bois-Brûlés, 1978, pp. 205-224.

Kubesh, Donald Arthur. "Ontario Press Reaction to the Northwest Rebellion of 1885." *Documentary Problems in Canadian History.* Vol. 2. Ed. J.M. Bumstead. Georgetown, Ontario: Irwin - Dorsey Limited, 1969, pp. 95 -128.

Lussier, Antoine S. "The Métis." *The Other Natives, the - les Métis, 1700 -1885.* Vol. 1. Eds. Antoine S. Lussier and D. Bruce Sealey. Winnipeg: Manitoba Métis Federation Press and Editions Bois-Brûlés, 1978, pp. 15 - 25.

Morton, A. S. "The New Nation, The Métis." *The Other Natives, the - les Métis, 1700 - 1885.* Vol. 1. Eds. Antoine S. Lussier and D. Bruce Sealey. Winnipeg: Manitoba Métis Federation Press and Editions Bois-Brûlés, 1978, pp. 27 - 37. (originally published in the *Royal Society of Canada Transactions,* 1939)

Morton, W. L. "The West and the Nation, 1870 - 1970." *Prairie Perspectives 2: Selected Papers of the Western Canadian Studies Conferences, 1970, 1971.* Eds. A. W. Rasporich and H. C. Klassen. Toronto: Holt, Rinehart and Winston, 1973, pp. 8 - 24.

Pannekoek, Frits. "The Anglican Church and the Disintegration of Red River Society, 1818 - 1870." *The West and the Nation: Essays in Honour of W. L. Morton.* Eds. Carl Berger and Ramsay Cook. Toronto: McClelland and Stewart, 1976, pp. 72 - 90.

————. "A Probe into the Demographic Structure of Nineteenth Century Red River." *Essays on Western History, in Honour of Lewis Gwynne Thomas.* Ed. Lewis H. Thomas. Edmonton: University of Alberta Press, 1976, pp. 83 - 95.

————. "The Rev. James Evans and the Social Antagonisms of the Fur Trade Society, 1840 - 1846." *Canadian Plains Studies 3: Religion and Society in the Prairie West.* Ed. Richard Allen. Regina: Canadian Plains Research Center, 1974, pp. 1 - 18.

Prud'homme, L.-A. "Notes Historiques sur les Métis du Nord-Ouest." *The Other Natives, the - les Métis, 1700 - 1885.* Vol. 1. Eds. Antoine S. Lussier and D. Bruce Sealey. Winnipeg: Manitoba Métis Federation Press and Editions Bois-Brûlés, 1978, pp. 87 - 113. (originally published in *Riel et la naissance du Manitoba,* 1921)

Silver, Arthur. "French Quebec and the Métis Question, 1869 - 1885." *The West and the Nation: Essays in Honour of W. L. Morton.* Eds. Carl Berger and Ramsay Cook. Toronto: McClelland and Stewart, 1976, pp. 91 - 113.

Stanley, George F. G. "Gabriel Dumont's Account of the North West Rebellion, 1885." *The Other Natives, the - les Métis, 1700 - 1885.* Vol 1. Eds. Antoine S. Lussier and D. Bruce Sealey. Winnipeg: Manitoba Métis Federation Press and Editions Bois-Brûlés, 1978, pp. 147 - 175. (originally published in *Canadian Historical Review,* 1949)

————. "The Half-breed 'Rising' of 1875." *The Other Natives, the - les Métis, 1700 - 1885.* Vol. 1. Eds. Antoine S. Lussier and D. Bruce Sealey. Winnipeg: Manitoba Métis Federation Press and Edition Bois-Brûlés, 1978, pp. 131 - 145. (originally published in *Canadian Historical Review,* 1936)

————. "Louis Riel." *Canada's Past and Present: A Dialogue.* Ed. Robert L. McDougall. Toronto: University of Toronto Press, 1965, pp. 21 - 40.

————. "The Western Canadian Mystique." *Prairie Perspectives: Papers of the Western Canadian Studies Conference.* Ed. David P. Gagan. Toronto: Holt, Rinehart and Winston, 1970, pp. 6 - 27.

Thomas, Lewis G. "Prairie Settlement: Western Responses in History and Fiction, Social Structures in a Canadian Hinterland." *Crossing Frontiers: Papers in American and Canadian Western Literature.* Ed. Dick Harrison. Edmonton: University of Alberta Press, 1979, pp. 59 - 72.

Thomas, Lewis H. "Government and Politics in Manitoba and the North West Territories." *The Prairie West to 1905: A Canadian Sourcebook.* Ed. Lewis G. Thomas. Toronto: Oxford University Press, 1975, pp. 73 - 130.

————. "A Judicial Murder - The Trial of Louis Riel." *The Settlement of the West.* Ed. Howard Palmer. Calgary: University of Calgary, Comprint Publishing Company, 1977, pp. 37 - 59.

General Books and Pamphlets

Abrams, Gary William David. "Loyalty in Adversity, 1884." and "The Rebellion and Its Aftermath, 1885." *Prince Albert: The First Century 1866 -1966.* Saskatoon: Modern Press, 1966, pp. 59 - 71, 72 - 82.

Adams, Howard Joseph. *Prison of Grass: Canada from the Native Point of View.* Toronto: New Press, 1975. 238 pp.

Allan, Iris Constance. *White Sioux: Major Walsh of the Mounted Police.* Sidney, B.C.: Gray's Publishing, 1969, 209 pp.

Anderson, Daniel R. and Alda M. (Anderson). *The Métis People of Canada: A History.* (Edmonton): The Alberta Federation of Métis Settlement Associations, n.d. 128 pp.

Andrist, Ralph K. *The Long Death; The Last Days of the Plains Indian.* New York: Collier-Macmillan, 1964. 371 pp.

Atkin, Ronald. *Maintain the Right: The Early History of the North West Mounted Police.* Toronto: Macmillan, 1973, 400 pp.

Batoche National Historic Site. Ottawa: Queen's Printer, 1965. 19 pp. (issued by the Minister of Indian Affairs and Northern Development)

Batten, Jack. *Canada Moves Westward: 1880 - 1890.* Toronto: Natural Science of Canada Limited, 1977. 128 pp. (Canada's Illustrated Heritage)

Beck, J. Murray. "'The Corpse of Riel' and National Unity." *Pendulum of Power: Canada's Federal Elections.* Scarborough, Ontario: Prentice-Hall, 1968, pp. 46 - 55.

Bergeron, Léandre. "Riel." *Petit manuel d'histoire du Québec.* 5ième ed. (Montréal): Editions Québécoises, n.d. pp. 147 - 170.

Berton, Pierre. *The Last Spike: The Great Railway 1881 - 1885.* Toronto: McClelland and Stewart, 1971. 478 pp.

———. *The National Dream: The Great Railway, 1871 - 1881.* Toronto: McClelland and Stewart, 1970. 439 pp.

Bliss, J.M., ed. "The West and Louis Riel." *Canadian History in Documents, 1763 — 1966.* Toronto: Ryerson Press, 1966. pp. 158 - 173.

Bowsfield, Hartwell, ed. *The James Wickes Taylor Correspondence, 1859 - 1870.* Vol 3. Altona, Manitoba: Manitoba Record Society Publications, 1968. 193pp.

Careless, J.M.S. *Brown of "The Globe": Statesman of Confederation 1860 - 1880.* Vol. 2. Toronto: Macmillan, 1963. 406pp.

———. *Canada: A Story of Challenge.* 3rd ed. Toronto: Macmillan, 1970. 449pp.

———, and R. Craig Brown, eds. *The Canadians 1867 - 1967.* 2nd ed. Toronto: Macmillan, 1969. 856pp.

Cashman, Tony. "Confrontation on Red River." "Northwest Rebellion." and "Riel: The Last Act." *An Illustrated History of Western Canada.* Edmonton: Hurtig Publishers, 1971, pp. 84 - 89, 117 - 128, 129 - 133.

Chafe, J. W. "The Riel Resistance and the Creation of the Province 1860 - 1870." *Extraordinary Tales from Manitoba History.* Toronto: McClelland and Stewart, 1973, pp. 79 - 95. (The Manitoba Historical Society)

Champagne, Antoine, ed. *Petite Histoire du voyageur.* Avant-propos de Lionel Dorge. Saint-Boniface: La Société historique de Saint-Boniface, 1971. 63pp.

Cook, Ramsay, John C. Ricker and John T. Saywell. "Railways, Riel and Sectionalism." *Canada: A Modern Study.* Toronto: Clarke, Irwin and Company, 1963, pp. 117 - 131. (Contemporary Canada: Issues and Insights)

Costisella, Joseph. "La Révolte des Métis: Louis Riel." et "Ils ont assassiné Louis Riel: insurrection de Batoche." *Le Peuple de la nuit: histoire des Québecois.* Montréal: Edition Chénier, 1965, pp. 81 - 88, 89 - 95.

MacLeod, Margaret, and W. L. Morton. *Cuthbert Grant of Grantown.* Toronto: McClelland and Stewart, 1974. 174pp. (Carleton Library No. 71)

McPherson, Arlean. *The Battlefords: A History.* Saskatoon: Modern Press, 1967. 264pp.

Martin, Chester. *"Dominion Lands" Policy.* Introd. Lewis H. Thomas. Toronto: McClelland and Stewart, 1973. 259pp. (Carleton Library No. 69)

Montizambert, Nancy. "Riel and the Métis." *Canada: The Prairie Provinces.* Toronto: McGraw-Hill, 1966, pp. 55 - 60.

Morton, Arthur S. *A History of the Canadian West to 1870 - 71...* Ed. Lewis G. Thomas. 2nd ed. Toronto: University of Toronto Press, 1973. 1039pp.

Morton, W.L. *The Critical Years: The Union of British North America 1857 - 1873.* Toronto: McClelland and Stewart, 1964. 322pp. (The Canadian Centenary Series)

————., ed. *Manitoba: The Birth of a Province.* Altona, Manitoba: Manitoba Record Society Publications, 1965. 265pp.

————. *Manitoba: A History.* 2nd ed. Toronto: University of Toronto Press, 1967. 547pp.

————. *The West and Confederation, 1857 - 1871.* Ottawa: Canadian Historical Association, 1968. 20pp. (Canadian Historical Association Booklets No. 9)

Neering, Rosemary. *North-West Mounted Police.* Toronto: Fitzhenry and Whiteside. 1974. 64pp. (Growth of a Nation Series)

————. *Settlement of the West.* Toronto: Fitzhenry and Whiteside, 1974. 64pp. (Growth of a Nation Series)

Newman, Lena. "Riel: Macdonald's Worst Blunder? - Stormy Rebel Splits English and French." *The John A. Macdonald Album.* Montreal: Tundra Books, 1974, pp. 102 - 109.

Osborne, Kenneth. "Annexation and Insurrection." "The 1885 Rebellion." *The Prairies: Selected Historical Sources.* Toronto: McClelland and Stewart, 1969, pp. 53 - 59, 60 - 69. (Curriculum Resource Books)

Paterson, T. W. *Canadian Battles and Massacres.* Langley, B.C.: Stagecoach Publishing Company, 1977, pp. 215 - 237.

Paterson, E. Palmer. *The Canadian Indian: A History Since 1500.* Don Mills, Ontario: Collier-Macmillan, 1972. 210pp.

Peel, Bruce. *Early Printing in the Red River Settlement 1859 - 1870: and Its Effect on the Riel Rebellion.* Winnipeg: Peguis, 1974. 56pp.

————. *Steamboats on the Saskatchewan.* Saskatoon: Western ·Poducer Prairie Books, 1972. 238pp.

Pelletier, Emile. *A Social History of the Manitoba Métis: The Development and Loss of Aboriginal Rights.* Winnipeg, Manitoba Métis Federation Press, 1974. 150pp.

Rasky, Frank. *The Taming of the Canadian West.* Toronto: McClelland and Stewart, 1967. 270pp.

Robertson, R.W.W. *The Execution of Thomas Scott.* Toronto: Burns MacEachern, 1968. 50pp. (Adventures in Canadian History)

Rodney, William. *Kootenai Brown: His Life and Times, 1839 - 1916.* Sidney, B.C.: Gray's Publishing, 1969. 251pp.

Rumilly, Robert. *Honoré Mercier et son temps.* Tome 1 (1840 - 1888), Tome 2 (1888 - 1894). Montréal: Fides, 1975. 418pp. (Vies Canadiennes)

Russell, R.C. *The Carlton Trail: The Broad Highway Into the Saskatchewan Country from the Red River Settlement, 1840 - 1880.* 2nd ed. Saskatoon: Western Producer Prairie Books, 1971. 158pp.

Sawchuk, Joe. *The Métis of Manitoba: Reformulation of an Ethnic Identity.* Toronto: Peter Martin Associates, 1978. 96pp. (Canadian Experience Series)

Saywell, John T., and John C. Ricker, eds. *Nation Making: Original Documents on the Founding of the Canadian Nation and the Settlement of the West, 1867 - 1885.* Toronto: Burns and MacEachern, 1967. 190pp.

Schull, Joseph. *Edward Blake: The Man of the Other Way, 1833 - 1881.* Vol. 1. Toronto: Macmillan, 1975. 257pp.

————. *Laurier: The First Canadian.* Toronto: Macmillan, 1965, pp. 79 - 199.

Sealey, Dawn. "Louis Riel, Jr. (1844 - 1885)." *Famous Manitoba Métis.* Ed. Bruce Sealey. Winnipeg: Manitoba Métis Federation Press, 1974, pp 51 -59.

Sealey, D. Bruce, and Antoine S. Lussier. *The Métis: Canada's Forgotten People.* Winnipeg: Manitoba Métis Federation Press, 1975. 200pp.

Shrive, Norman. "Red River: Insurrection." *Charles Mair, Literary Nationalist.* Toronto: University of Toronto Press, 1965. pp. 83 - 121.

Silver, A. I., and Marie France Valeur. *The North-West Rebellion: Suggestions for the Teacher.* n.p., n.d. 12pp.

Skelton, Oscar Douglas. "The Mackenzie Administration." "Rail and Riel." *Life and Letters of Sir Wilfred Laurier.* Vol. 1. Toronto: McClelland and Stewart, 1965. pp. 49 - 65, 75 - 98. (Carleton Library No. 21)

Sluman, Norma. *Poundmaker.* Toronto: Ryerson Press, 1967. 301pp.

Stanley, George F. G. *Manitoba 1870: une réalisation métisse/A Métis Achievement.* Winnipeg: University of Winnipeg Press, 1972. 30pp.

Swainson, Donald. *John A. Macdonald: The Man and the Politician.* Toronto: Oxford University Press, 1971. 160pp.

———. *Macdonald of Kingston: First Prime Minister.* Toronto: Personal Library Publishers, 1979. (Canada's Heritage in Pictures)

Tanner, Ogden. *The Old West: The Canadians.* Alexandria, Virginia: Time-Life Books, 1977. 240pp.

Thomas, Lewis H. *The North-West Territories 1870 - 1905.* Ottawa: Canadian Historical Association, 1970. 24pp. (Canadian Historical Booklets No. 26)

———. *The Struggle for Responsible Government in the North-West Territories 1870 - 1897.* 2nd ed. Toronto: University of Toronto Press, 1978. 304pp.

Wade, Mason. "Riel, The West, and Mercier: 1818 - 1897." *The French Canadians, 1760 - 1911.* Vol. 1. rev. ed. Toronto: Macmillan, 1968, pp. 393 -446.

Waite, Peter B. *Canada, 1874 - 1896: Arduous Destiny.* Toronto: McClelland and Stewart, 1971. 340pp. (Canadian Centenary Series No. 13)

Woodcock, George. *Canada and the Canadians.* Toronto: Oxford University Press, 1970. 344pp.

———. *Gabriel Dumont.* Don Mills, Ontario: Fitzhenry and Whiteside, 1978. 63pp.

Theses

Abrams, Gary William David. "A History of Prince Albert, Saskatchewan, to 1914." M.A. Diss. Univ. of Saskatchewan 1965.

Bartlett, R. E. "William Mactavish: the last Governor of Assiniboia." M.A. Diss. Univ. of Manitoba 1964.

Bingaman, Sandra. "The North West Rebellion Trials, 1885." M.A. Diss. Univ. of Saskatchewan (Regina) 1971.

Brown, R. C. "Canadian-American Relations in the Latter Part of the Nineteenth Century." Ph. D. Diss. Univ. of Toronto 1963.

Carr, Sheila Betty. "New Brunswick Reaction to the North West Rebellion: A Study in Regionalism and Ethnicity." M.A. Diss. Univ. of New Brunswick 1971.

Carter, Sarah A. "Perceptions of the Canadian North West in the Eighteen-Fifties." M.A. Diss. Univ. of Saskatchewan 1976.

Chambers, B. "Politics and Psychiatry: Louis Riel." M.D. Diss. Univ. of Calgary 1971.

Comeault, G. L. "The Political Impact of Archbishop Langevin." M.A. Diss. Univ. of Manitoba 1972.

Degehr, T. D. "The National Railway Policy and Manitoba Railway Legislation, 1879-1889." M.A. Diss. Carleton Univ. 1964.

Désilets, Andrée. "Un Père de la Confédération canadienne, Hector-Louis Langevin, 1826 - 1906." Ph. D. Diss. Laval Univ. 1968.

Devrome, Robert J. "The Métis: Colonization: Culture Change and The Saskatchewan Rebellion of 1885." M.A. Diss. Univ. of Alberta 1976.

Dunn, J. "The Alberta Field Force of 1885." M.A. Diss. Univ. of Calgary 1975.

Foster, John Elgin. "The Anglican Clergy in the Red River Settlement, 1820 -1826." M.A. Diss. Univ. of Alberta 1966.

———. "The Country-Born in the Red River Settlement, 1820 - 1850." Ph. D. Diss. Univ. of Alberta 1973.

Graham, Jane Elizabeth. "The Riel Amnesty and the Liberal Party in Central Canada, 1869 - 1875." M.A. Diss. Queen's Univ. 1967.

Hecht, Irene. "Annexation and the Red River Rebellion of 1869 - 70." Ph. D. Diss. Univ. of Washington 1965.

Huel, R.J.A. "L'Association catholique franco-canadienne de la Saskatchewan: A Response to Cultural Assimilation." M.A. Diss. Univ. of Saskatchewan (Regina) 1969.

———. "La Survivance in Saskatchewan: Schools, Politics and the Nativist Crusade for Cultural Conformity." Ph. D. Diss. Univ. of Alberta 1975.

Jahn, Hertha Evelyn. "Immigration and Settlement in Manitoba, 1870 - 1881; the beginnings of a pattern." M.A. Diss. Univ. of Manitoba 1968.

Jamieson, R.T. "Some Aspects of John A. Macdonald's Attitudes and Policies Towards the Canadian West, 1871 - 1891." M.A. Diss. Guelph Univ. 1971.

Klassen, H.C. "The Red River Settlement and the St. Paul Route 1859 -1870." M.A. Diss. Univ. of Manitoba 1963.

Lague, G. "L'Opinion de la presse anglaise sur l'affaire Louis Riel." M.A. Diss. Univ. de Sherbrooke 1973.

Lalonde, André N. "Settlement in the North West Territories by colonization companies, 1881 - 1891." Ph. D. Diss. Laval Univ. 1970.

Larmour, Jean. "Edgar Dewdney, Commissioner of Indian Affairs and Lieutenant-Governor of the North-West Territories, 1879 - 1888." M.A. Diss. Univ. of Saskatchewan (Regina) 1969.

Lavallée, André. "La Rébellion de 1885 dans le Nord-Ouest Canadien; les réactions canadiennes et 'Canadian'." Diss. Univ. de Montréal 1966.

Looy, A.J. "The Indian Agent and his Role in the Administration of the North-West Superintendency, 1876 - 1893." Ph. D. Diss. Queen's Univ. 1972.

McAlduff, Maureen. "Joseph Dubuc; Role and Views of a French Canadian in Manitoba, 1870 - 1914." M.A. Diss. Ottawa Univ. 1967.

McCarty, R.F. "Fort Assiniboine, Alberta, 1823 - 1913: fur tradepost to settled district." Diss. Univ. of Alberta 1976.

McPherson, Arlean Esther. "A History of the Battlefords to 1914." M.A. Diss. Univ. of Saskatchewan 1966.

Martel, Gilles. "Louis Riel: Les Années de formation." M.A. Diss. Univ. de Sherbrooke 1972.

———. "Le Messianisme de Louis Riel (1844 - 1885)." Thèse de doctorat. Paris, Ecole des hautes études en sciences sociales 1976.

Mitchner, Ernest Alyn. "William Pearce and Federal Activity in Western Canada, 1882 - 1904." Ph. D. Diss. Univ. of Alberta 1971.

Morgan, Edwin Charles. "The North-West Mounted Police, 1873 - 1883." M.A. Diss. Univ. of Saskatchewan (Regina)1970.

Overholtzer, H. "James Wickes Taylor as U.S. Consul in Winnipeg, 1870 -1893." Ph. D. Diss. McMaster Univ. 1972.

Painchaud, Robert. "Le Manitoba et l'immigration canadienne-française, 1870 - 1891." M.A. Diss. Univ. d'Ottawa 1969.

———. "The Catholic Church and the Movement of Francophones to the Canadian Prairies, 1870 - 1915." Ph. D. Diss. Ottawa Univ. 1976.

Pannekoek, Fritz. "Protestant Agricultural Missions in the Canadian West to 1870." M.A. Diss. Univ. of Alberta 1970.

———. "The Churches and the Social Structure in the Red River Area 1818 - 1870." Ph. D. Diss. Queen's Univ. 1973.

Payment, Diane Paulette, "Le Rôle des Métis de la Riveéè-Rouge dans le conseil d'Assiniboia, 1832 - 1869." M.A. Diss. Univ. d'Ottawa 1974.

Pilon, Conrad. "French Canadian Settlement in Manitoba, 1870 - 1890." M.A. Diss. Univ. of Manitoba 1972.

Sawchuk, Joe. "The Metis of Manitoba." M.A. Diss. Univ. of Manitoba 1972.

Sealey, Gary David. "History of the Hudson's Bay Company, 1870 - 1900." M.A. Diss. Univ. of Western Ontario 1970.

Semotuk, Lydia Nancy. "The Hudson's Bay Company as a Political Institution." M.A. Diss. Univ. of Alberta 1971.

Silver, Arthur Isaac. "French-Canadian Attitudes Toward the North-West and North-West Settlement, 1870 - 1890." M.A. Diss. McGill Univ. 1966.

———. "Quebec and the French-Speaking Minorities, 1864 - 1917." Ph. D. Diss. Univ. of Toronto 1973.

Slauenwhite, Margaret Rose. "Confederation and the Manifest Destiny of the British North West." B.A. (Honours) Acadia Univ. 1967.

Smith, Carl Franklin. "Louis Riel; a false prophet." B.A. (Honours) Acadia Univ. 1967.

Sprenger, G. Herman. "An Analysis of Selective Aspects of Metis Society, 1810 - 1870." M.A. Diss. Univ. of Manitoba 1972.

Taylor, John Leonard. "Law and Order at Red River." M.A. Diss. Carleton Univ. 1967.

Ward, William Peter. "The Administration of Justice in the North-West Territories, 1870 - 1887." M.A. Diss. Univ. of Alberta 1966.

Wright, Helen. "Louis Riel Père and the French Struggle for Political Rights in Red River, 1838 - 1858." Diss. Univ. of Manitoba 1963.

Facsimile Editions

Chambers, Ernest J. "The Rebellion of 1885." *The Royal North-West Mounted Police: A Corps History.* Toronto: Coles Publishing Company, 1972, pp. 81 - 102. (Coles Canadiana Collection) (originally published in Montreal: Mortimer Press, 1906)

Corbett, Rev. G.O. *Notes on Rupert's Land.* Introd. Bruce Peel. Toronto Bibliographical Society of Canada, 1967. 88pp. (Facsimile Series No. 8) (originally published in London: 1868)

Dawson, Simon James. *The Red River Expedition of 1870.* Toronto: Canadiana Library Service, 1967. 22pp. (reprinted from the *Thunder Bay Sentinel* of September 21st 1882)

Deane, R. Burton. *Mounted Police Life in Canada: A Record of Thirty-One Years' Service.* Toronto: Coles Publishing Company, 1973. 311pp. (Coles Canadiana Collection) (originally published in Toronto: Cassell and Company, 1916)

Denny, Cecil Edward Sir. *The Last Marches West.* Ed. W.B. Cameron. Toronto: J.M. Dent and Sons, 1972. 319pp. (originally published in London: Dent, 1939)

Donkin, John G. *Trooper and Redskin in the Far North-West: Recollections of Life in the North-West Mounted Police, Canada, 1884 - 1888.* Toronto: Coles Publishing Company, 1973. 289 pp. (Coles Canadiana Collection) (originally published in London: Sampson Low, Marston, Searle and Rivington, 1889)

Haydon, A.L. *The Riders of the Plains: A Record of the Royal North-West Mounted Police of Canada, 1873 - 1910.* Edmonton: Hurtig Publishers, 1971. 385pp. (originally published in London, 1910)

MacBeth, Rev. R.G. *The Making of the Canadian West, being the Reminiscences of an Eye-Witness.* Toronto: Coles Publishing Company, 1973. 230pp. (Coles Canadiana Collection) (originally published in Toronto: William Briggs, 1898)

Morris, Alexander. *The Treaties of Canada with the Indians of Manitoba and the North West Territories...* Toronto: Coles Publishing Company, 1971. 375pp. (Coles Canadiana Collection) (originally published in Toronto: Belfords, Clarke and Company, 1880)

Morton, W.L., ed. *Alexander Begg's Red River Journal and Other Papers Relative to the Red River Resistance of 1869 - 1870.* facs. ed. New York: Greenwood Press Publishers, 1969. 636pp. (originally published in Toronto: The Champlain Society, 1956 (Champlain Society Publication, No. 34)

Mulvaney, Charles Pelham. *The History of the North-West Rebellion of 1885.* Toronto: Coles Publishing Company, 1971. 424pp. (Coles Canadiana Collection) (originally published in Toronto: A.H. Hovey and Company, 1885)

Ross, Alexander. *The Red River Settlement; its rise, progress, and present state,...* Introd. W.L. Morton. Edmonton: Hurtig Publishers, 1972. 416pp. (originally published in London: Smith, Elder, 1856)

Steele, Samuel B. *Forty Years in Canada: Reminiscences of the Great North-West with some Account of his Service in South Africa.* Toronto: McGraw-Hill Ryerson, 1972. 464pp. (originally published in Toronto: McClelland, Goodchild and Stewart, 1914)

The Story of Louis Riel: The Rebel Chief. Toronto: Coles Publishing Company, 1979. 192 pp. (Coles Canadiana Collection) (originally published in Toronto: J.S. Robertson and Brothers, 1885).

Literary Texts

Anonymous. "The Charge at Batoche." In *The Poets' Record: Verses on Canadian History*. Eds. Keith Wilson and Elva Motheral. Winnipeg: Peguis, pp. 56 - 57.

Cameron, William Bleasdell. *Blood Red the Sun*. Edmonton: Hurtig Publishers, 1977. (originally published in 1926 and entitled *The War Trail of Big Bear)*

Campbell, Maria. *Halfbreed*. Toronto: McClelland and Stewart, 1973. (Dumont and Riel used as a leitmotiv)

Carefoot, E.H. *Gabriel Dumont at Batoche*. Saskatoon: (Craft Litho), 1973. 38pp. (poetry)

Charette, Guillaume. *L'Espace de Louis Goulet*. Winnipeg: Editions Bois-Brûlés, 1976.

Coulter, John. *The Crime of Louis Riel*. Toronto: Playwrights Co-op, 1976. (the third play in the Riel trilogy)

———. Riel. *(A Play in Two Parts)* Hamilton, Ontario: Cromlech Press, 1972. 142pp.

———. *The Trial of Louis Riel*. Ottawa: Oberon Press, 1968.

———. *The Trial of Louis Riel*. Trans. Raynald Desmeules. Ottawa: Oberon Press, 1968. 66pp.

Cutt, W. Towrie. *On the Trail of Long Tom*. Toronto: Collins, 1970. (the life story of a young Cree in 1880)

Everson, R.G. "Two Poems." *Mosaic,* 3, No. 3 (Spring 1970), 127 - 128. (short poems on Riel)

Gutteridge, Don. "The Buffalo Hunt." *Mosaic,* 3, No. 3 (Spring 1970), 118 -122. (excerpt from his poem Riel)

————. "Riel. (Beauport Asylum, January 1878)" In *The Poets' Record: Verses on Canadian History*. Eds. Keith Wilson and Elva Motheral. Winnipeg: Peguis, 1975, pp. 54 - 56. (excerpts from the poem Riel)

————. *Riel; A Poem for Voices*. Toronto: Van Nostrand Reinhold, 1972. 73pp.

Harrison, Dick, ed. "The North-West Rebellion and After." *Best Mounted Police Stories*. Edmonton: University of Alberta Press, 1978, pp. 61 -159.

Lutz, Giles A. *The Magnificent Failure*. Toronto: Doubleday Canada Limited, 1967. 330pp. (adventure novel precisely on Riel and Dumont)

McNamee, James. *Them damn Canadians hanged Louis Riel!* Toronto: Macmillan, 1971. 133pp. (parts of the novel published in 1962 under the title *My Uncle Joe)*

Reekie, Isabel M. *Red, Horse of the West*. Toronto: Holt, Rinehart and Winston, 1971. (fiction for the young)

Richard, Jean-Jules. *Exovide: Louis Riel*. Montréal: Les Editions La Presse, 1970. 260pp.

Rosenstock, Janet and Dennis Adair. *Riel*. Markham, Ontario: PaperJacks, 1979. (text based on original screenplay by Roy Moore)

Sanderson, James F. *Indian Tales of the Canadian Prairies*. (1894) Calgary: Historical Society of Alberta, 1965. 16pp. (the author was a prisoner of Riel)

Saunders, Thomas. *Red River of the North and Other Poems of Manitoba*. Winnipeg: Peguis, 1969.

Stegner, Wallace. *Wolf Willow: A History, A Story, and A Memory of the Last Plains Frontier*. Toronto: Macmillan, 1977. 306pp. (Laurentian Library, 59) (there are many references to Riel in this classic which was originally published in 1955)

Souster, Raymond. "Riel, 16 Novembre, 1885." In *The Poets' Record: Verses on Canadian History*. Eds. Keith Wilson and Elva Motheral. Winnipeg: Peguis, 1975, p.58.

Truss, Jan. *A Very Small Rebellion*. Introd. Jack Chambers. Edmonton: J.M. LeBel Enterprises, 1977. (juvenile fiction)

Walsh, Frederick G. *The Trial of Louis Riel*. Fargo, N.D.: North Dakota Institute for Regional Studies, 1965. (drama)

Weibe, Rudy. *The Scorched-Wood People*. Toronto: McClelland and Stewart, 1977. 351pp.

———. *The Temptations of Big Bear*. Toronto: McClelland and Stewart, 1973. 415pp.

Woodcock, George. *Gabriel Dumont and the Northwest Rebellion*. Toronto: Playwrights Co-op, 1976. 32pp.

Footnotes

Louis Riel's Name "David"

Abbreviations

AASB	Archives de l'Archevêché de St.-Boniface
ACAM	Archives de la Chancellerie de l'Archidiocèce de Montréal
ASQ	Archives du Séminaire du Québec
ASTR	Archives du Séminaire de Trois-Rivières
AUNB	Archives of the University of New Brunswick
PAC	Public Archives of Canada
PAM	Provincial Archives of Manitoba

1. Oct. 22 appears in a statement by Riel's mother. (PAM), Riel collection, No. 599. Riel gave Oct. 23 in his autobiographical "Compte - Rendu de ses activités," AASB.
2. Published in G. Martel, G. Campbell, T. Flanagan, *Louis Riel: Poésies de jeunesse* (St. Boniface, 1977), pp. 149-156.
3. G.F. Stanley, *Louis Riel* (Toronto, 1963), pp. 191-195.
4. Joseph Debuc to Louis Riel, Oct. 17, 1873: PAM, Riel Collection, No. 220.
5. E.P. Lachapelle to Louis Riel, Jan. 29, 1874. *Ibid.,* No. 237.
6. Interview with Riel, *Montreal Star,* Aug. 22, 1885: PAM, Riel Collection, No. 599.
7. Peter Charlebois, *The Life of Louis Riel* (Toronto, 1975), p. 104.
8. H. Bowsfield (ed.), "Louis Riel's Letter to President Grant, 1875,"*Saskatchewan History,* 21 (1968).
9. See T. Flanagan, *Louis "David" Riel: "Prophet of the New World"* (Toronto, 1979), passim.
10. Dossier No. 565 in the medical archives of the Centre Hospitalier Saint-Jean-de-Dieu (Montréal-Gamelin).
11. Henry Howard, "Medical History of Louis David Riel during his Detention in Longue Pointe Asylum," *Canada Medical and Surgical Journal,* June, 1886), 641-41.

12. *Ibid.*
13. *Ibid.*
14. Louis Riel to Ignace Bourget, April 20 and May 1, 1876. ACAM.
15. Joseph Dubuc, "Mémoires d'un Manitobain," ms., PAM.
16. Riel to Bourget, May 1, 1876. ACAM.
17. *Ibid.*
18. *Ibid.*
19. Hôpital St-Michel-Archange (Beauport), Dossier No. 3697; "Larochelle" is mentioned in PAC, Ministry of Justice, Records Relating to Louis Riel and the North-West Uprising, 1873-1886, 217-18, which is an affidavit from the Provincial Secretary of Quebec, June 21, 1885
20 ASQ. Riel Papers, pp. 109.
21. The question is discussed in Flanagan, *op. cit.,* pp.84-86.
22. PAM, Riel Family Papers.
23. ASQ, Riel Papers, pp. 97-98.
24. Several places, with minor variations, in ASQ, Riel Papers.
25. *Ibid.,* p.144.
26. Louis Riel to Ignace Bourget (draft), February, 1884. PAC, Justice Records, 63-69.
27. J.W. Schultz, *My Life as an Indian* (New York, 1907), p. 382.
28. Louis Riel to A. -A. Taché, n.d. ASTR.
29. Marriage certificate, SHSB.
30. Louis Riel to A.-A. Taché (draft), n.d. PAC, Justice Records, p. 38.
31. *Ibid.* There is no version of this letter in ASB, where Riel's letters to Taché were conserved.
32. E.G. Desmond Morton (ed.), *The Queen v Louis Riel* (Toronto, 1974), trial exhibits 5, 9, 14, 17, 19, 20, pp. 373-382.
33. T. Flanagan (ed.), *The Diaries of Louis Riel* (Edmonton, 1976), pp. 68-69.
34. *The Queen v. Louis Riel,* p. 352.
35. A copy of the abjuration in Fourmond's hand, dated Aug. 5, 1885, is in ASB; Riel's own copy, with his name "David" added and dated Aug. 4, 1885, is in AUNB.
36. *Diaries of Louis Riel,* p. 134.
37. See in general V. Lanternari, *Religions of the Oppressed* (New York, 1963).

The Metis:
The People and the Term

1. Joe Sawchuk, *The Métis of Manitoba,* Toronto, 1978, contains an excellent discussion of this development as it relates currently to Manitoba.
2. See particularly J. Russell Harper (ed.), *Paul Kane's Frontier,* Toronto, 1971, pp. 86, 142, 188, 189, 190, 191.
3. See Alexander Ross, *The Red River Settlement,* London, 1856, reprinted Minneapolis, 1956 and Edmonton, 1972, pp. 245-273.
4. See William Butler, *The Great Lone Land,* London, 1872, reprinted Edmonton, 1968, Appendix A, p. 386.
5. See Marcel Giraud, *Le Métis Canadien,* Paris, 1945, pp. 669-692 and E. E. Rich(ed.), *Eden Colvile's Letters, 1849-52,* London, 1956, Introduction by W.L. Morton. Professor Morton's introduction constitutes the most useful social history of the Red River Settlement in this period. As well, note J. E. Foster, "The Country-born in the Red River Settlement, 1820-1850" (Ph.D., Alberta, 1973).
6. See Giraud, pp. 1002-1041.
7. Trudy Nicks, "Iroquois and the Fur Trade in Western Canada" (unpublished paper, Fur Trade Conference, Winnipeg, 1978) constitutes the most recent and most useful scholarly study.
8. *Ibid.* p.15.
9. Jacqueline Peterson, "Prelude to Red River: A Social Portrait of the Great Lakes Métis." *Ethnohistory* Winter, 1977, XXIV, 1, note 3 (in press).
10. Jennifer S. H. Brown, "Halfbreed, Squaw, and Other Categories: Some Semantic Shifts and their Implications in the Northwest Fur Trade, 1800-1850" (unpublished paper, Fur Trade Conference, Winnipeg, 1978). Dr. Brown's study is fundamental to any discussion on terminology bearing on the "mixed-bloods" in Western history.
11. For an explanation of the reasons for the use of this term see J. E. Foster. "The Origins of the Mixed Bloods in the Canadian West" in L. H. Thomas(ed.). *Essays on Western History,* Edmonton, 1976, pp. 72-73. To date I have encountered "Rupert'slander" only in conversations with scholars seeking a more effective term for this socio-cultural entity.
12. J. M. S. Careless, "Frontierism, Metropolitanism and Canadian History," *Canadian Historical Review,* XXXV, 1, March, 1954, details the historical explanation that frequently evokes the metropolitan

perspective.

13. Perhaps the most useful examples are the scholarly treatments of Governor George Simpson. See A. S. Morton, *Sir George Simpson,* Toronto, 1944, and J. S. Galbraith, *The Little Emperor,* Toronto, 1976.

14. A. J. Ray, *Indians in the Fur Trade,* Toronto, 1974, pp. 59-61, 85.

15. C. W. Cole, *Colbert and a Century of French Mercantilism,* Hamden, 1939, 2 vols., and Eli F. Heckscher, *Mercantilism,* London, 1935, 2 vols., present effective studies of the relationship between "commercial interests" and "the national interest" in this period. Also see W. J. Eccles, *The Canadian Frontier,* Toronto, 1969, pp. 130-31.

16 Eccles, p. 116.

17. R. J. Surtees, "The Development of an Indian Reserve Policy in Canada," in J. K. Johnson(ed.) *Historical Essays on Upper Canada,* Toronto, 1975, p. 262.

18. Giraud, pp. 312-331. Also see the Peterson article.

19. Eccles, p. 190.

20. *Ibid.,* pp. 55, 57, 59.

21. *Ibid.,* pp. 126, 131, 146-149.

22. Grace L. Nute, *The Voyageur,* New York, 1931, reprinted St. Paul, 1955, p. 93.

23. Pierre Gualtier de Varennes, Sieur de la Verendrye and his sons and nephews are perhaps the most familiar example. As well see Peterson.

24. A quick perusal of E. E. Rich, *Simpson's Athabasca Journal,* "Introduction" by Chester Martin, London, 1938, and materials in the Hudson's Bay Co. Archives such as the post journals, account books, and reports of the Athabasca country for the period 1800-1840 suggest politico-social strategies very similar to the Great Lakes trading families in an earlier period. Note particularly H.B.C.A., B. 239/Z/12, York Factory Miscellaneous Items, 1838.

25. The patronyms of several Métis families, such as Sayer, Wilkie, Pongman, McGillis and others attest to this development.

26. E. E. Rich, *The Fur Trade and the North West to 1857,* Toronto, 1967, p. 109.

27. *Ibid.*

28. Ray, pp. 59-61

29. J. E. Foster, "The Indian Trader in the Hudson Bay Fur Tradition," in J. Freedman and J. H. Barkow (eds.), *Proceedings of the Second Congress, Canadian Ethnology Society,* Ottawa, 1975, Vol. 11, p. 578.

30. Brown, p. 15.

31. *Ibid.*

32. H.B.C.A., A 16/32, "York Servants Accounts, 1738-60," fo. 19, fo. 20.

33. H.B.C.A., B. 239/a/49, "York Factory Journals," fo. 20, Jan, 2-3, 1762.

34. J.E. Foster. "The Home Guard Cree: The First Hundred Years" in D.A. Muise (ed.), *Approaches to Native History in Canada,* Ottawa, 1977, p. 59.

35. H.B.C.A., B. 239/a/49, "York Factory Journals," fo. 20, January 2-3, 1762.

36. *Ibid.*

37. Brown, p. 4.

38. *Ibid., pp. 10-11.*

39. Ross, P. 273.

40. A.S. Morton, "The New Nation, The Métis," *Transactions of the Royal Society of Canada,* Series III, Section 2, 1939, pp. 138-139.

41. Giraud, pp. 968-973.

42. Robert Gosman, *The Riel and Lagimodière Families in Métis Society, 1840-1860,* Ottawa, 1977, pp. 1-3.

43. Giraud, pp. 669-691, 1087.

44. Nicks, pp. 3-5.

45. *Ibid.,* p. 13.

46. *Ibid.,*pp. 14-15.

47. Brown, p. 4.

48. Foster, *The Country-born...,* pp. 157-163.

49. *Ibid.* p.203.

50. *Ibid.* p.184.

51. Church Missionary Society Archives, Incoming Correspondence, Joseph Cook to the Lay Secretary, 29 July, 1846.

52. Brown, pp. 8-9.

53. Public Archives of Canada, M.G. 17, B1, D 13, Society for the Propagation of the Gospel, Rupert's Land, 1850-59, Rev. D. T. Anderson to Rev. E. Hawkins, 24 November, 1852.

54. Brown, pp. 8-9.

55. P.A.C., M.G. 19, E6, Vol. 1, Thomas Cook to Rev. John Smithurst, January 30, 1853.

56. Foster, "Origins...," p. 72.

57. Brown, pp. 9-10.

58. *Ibid.* pp. 4-5, 9-10.

59. *Ibid.*

60. *Ibid.*

61. Glyndwr Williams (ed.), Hudson's Bay Miscellany, 1670-1870, Winnipeg, 1975, p. 227. Initially Simpson had serious reservations concerning Sinclair's abilities.

62. Perhaps the most familiar was Simpson's cousin Chief Trader Thomas Simpson. See Alexander Simpson, *Life and Travels,* London, 1845.

63. Foster, "Origins...," p. 79.

Louis Schmidt:
A Forgotten Metis

1. *Le Patriote de l'Ouest* (Prince Albert), 13 nov. 1935.
2. Published serially between June 1, 1911 and July 11, 1912.
3. Louis Schmidt, "Mémoires" (Mémoires), *Le Patriote de l'Ouest,* 8 juin 1911.
4. Oblate Archives, Provincial Archives of Alberta, C.II.103, "Baptêmes et Mariages dans les Missions des Forts des Prairies, 1842-51", No. 1201.
5. "Mémoires", 8 juin 1911.
6. Archives of the Archdiocese of St. Boniface (A.A. St. B.), Correspondance de Mgr Taché (Taché), Schmidt to Taché, 17 aôut 1861, T07774-775.
7. *Ibid.* 1 jan. 1862, T1088-089.
8. "Mémoires", 25 jan. 1912.
9. *Ibid.* 8 fév. 1912.
10. .A.A. St. B., Schmidt to Taché, 5 juin 1880, T23967-972. Schmidt to Taché, 11 sept. 1880, T24450.
11. *Ibid.,* 18 fév. 1884, T28831.
12. *Ibid.,* T28832.
13. Louis Schmidt, "Déclaration", 16 déc. 1909.
14. "Mémoires", 23 mai 1912.
15. George Woodcock, *Gabriel Dumont. The Métis Chief and His Lost World.* Hurtig, 1975, pp. 120 and 137.
16. A.A. St. B., Louis Schmidt, "Notes. Mouvement des Métis à St. Laurent, Sask. T.N.O. en 1884 (Notes), "T29781-840. See also Schmidt to Taché, 8 avril 1885, T31063.
17. "Déclaration", 16 dec 1909; "Notes", T29825-827.
18. A.A. St. B., "Notes", T29785-786.
19. *Ibid.,* T29789-790.
20. *Ibid.,* Schmidt to Taché, 8 avril 1885, T31065-066; "Notes", T29788.
21. *Ibid.,* "Notes", T29794.
22. *Ibid.,* Schmidt to Taché, 7 mars 1885, T30938.
23. *Ibid.,* "Notes", T29833.
24. *Ibid.,* Schmidt to Taché, 27 mai 1885, T31419-421.
25. *House of Commons Debates,* July 7, 1885, p. 3155.
26. Journal de Louis Schmidt, 7 juillet 1897.
27. *Ibid.,* 6 jan. 1903.

A Survey of
Louis Riel's Poetry.

*   I am indebted to the Social Sciences and Humanities Research Council of Canada and to the Calgary Institute for the Humanities for their support of the research presented here. I would like to thank also my colleague Thomas Flanagan and my research assistant Louise Westra for their help in the preparation of this material.

1.   *La Minerve,* June 5, 1885, p.3. The poems are addressed to "Notre Seigneur identifié avec son clergé", to the Sainte Vierge", and to "Sa Grandeur Monseigneur Taché".

2.   In a short note preceding verse which he wrote while imprisoned in Montana, in May, 1883, Riel make a request to Mr. Fisk, Editor of the *Helena Herald:* "Sir, you would oblige me a great deal in publishing those lines composed and written in my jail." (Public Archives of Canada (hereafter abbreviated as PAC), *Dept. of Justice Records,* Microfilm C-1229, p. 2365A.) In a poem dedicated to the "Rév. Père Jésuite Frédérick Ebersville", Riel writes:

> Car l'attention générale
> En devenant impartiale
> Mettra peut-être en vogue un jour mes vers fançais

(Poésies Religieuses et Politiques, p. 35). About his guards in the Regina jail, Riel had this hope:

> After a while, I wish the boys
> of the Mounted Police
> Would pile up the sum of my Joyce (sic)
> By publishing all my smal (sic) scrips.

(PAC, *Edgar Dewdney Papers,* microfilm C-4595, pp. 2137-2138).

3.   *L'Opinion publique,* February 19, 1870. Included in Prud'home's article are a fable "La Fourmi et sa mère", a song "A mes amis", and lines addressed to George Etienne Cartier. These works have been republished in *Louis Riel: Poésies de jeunesse* (see note 5).

4.   Louis "David" Riel, *Poésies Religieuses et Politiques* (Montreal, L'Etendard, 1886). This publication contains the following poems: "Mon Sauveur", "Notre Seigneur identifié avec son clergé", "La Sainte Vierge", "L'Archevêque de Saint-Boniface", "Joseph Damiani", "Au Rév. Père Jésuite Frédérick Ebersville", "A Sir John A. MacDonald", and "Reconnaissance".

5. *Louis Riel: Poésies de jeunesse* (Saint Boniface: Les Editions du Blé, 1977).
6. *Ibid.,* pp. 130-135.
7. Archives du Séminaire de Québec, *Louis Riel: Ecrit de Beauport,* p. 2. With the exception of accents which have been added when required, this text and those that follow have been printed exactly as the poet wrote them, i.e. the spelling, punctuation, capitalization (or lack thereof), etc., are Riel's.
8. *Ibid.*
9. Provincial Archives of Manitoba (hereafter abbreviated as PAM), *Riel Family Papers* (1966), MG3, D2, Box 3. This is a draft version of the poem addressed to Sir John A. MacDonald.
10. *Ibid.*
11. Harriet Irving Library, University of New Brunswick, *Louis Riel Papers.*
12. PAC, *Papers of Louis Riel,* MG27, IF3, Vol. 2, Item 44.
13. PAC, *Dept. of Justice Records,* microfilm C-1229, p. 2205.
14. PAC, *Papers of Louis Riel,* Item 42. This poem, under the title "A Sir John A. MacDonald" is found in *Poésies Religieuses et Politiques.*
    It is dated: Saint-Joseph, Dakota, August, 1879. There are numerous substantival variants between the manuscript and printed versions. Note Riel's spelling of "MacDonald".
15. PAM, *Riel Family Papers,* (1966).
16. PAC, *Dept. of Justice Records,* microfilm C-1229, pp. 2243-2244. This poem, with minor variants, is found in *Poésies Religieuses et Politiques.*
17. *Ibid.,* p. 2226.
18. This notebook is in the PAM, *Riel Family Papers* (1966), and was used as the chief manuscript source for *Louis Riel: Poésies de jeunesse.*
19. *Louis Riel: Poésies de jeunesse.* p. 119.
20. *Ibid.,* p. 101.
21. This matter has been discussed at greater length in the Introduction to *Louis Riel Poésies de jeunesse.*
22. PAM, *Riel Family Papers* (1966).
23. *Ibid.*
24. *Louis Riel: Poésies de jeunesse,* pp. 94-95.
25. See George F. G. Stanley, *Louis Riel* (Toronto: McGraw-Hill Ryerson Limited, 1972), p. 231.
26. PAM, *Riel Family Papers* (1966).
27. See Stanley, *op.cit.,* p.232.
28. Ibid., pp. 238-239. See also Joseph Kinsey Howard, *The Strange Empire of Louis Riel* (Toronto, Swan Publishing Co. Ltd., 1970), pp. 294-296.
29. PAM, *Louis Riel Collection,* MG3, D1, Document 528.
30. *Ibid.*
31. See Stanley, *op.cit.,* p. 239.

32. PAC, *Dept. of Justice Records,* microfilm C-1228, pp. 999-1000. The poem is also found, in a different hand, with several variants, in PAC, *Sir John A. Macdonald Papers,* microfilm C-1524, pp. 43186-43191.

33. PAC, *Dept. of Justice Records,* microfilm C-1229, p. 2338.

34. *Ibid.,* p. 2255.

35. *Ibid.,* p. 2365.

36. PAC, *Edgar Dewdney Papers,* microfilm C4595, p. 2134.

37. PAC, *Dept. of Justice Records,* microfilm C-1229, p. 23650.

38. PAM, *Riel Family Papers* (1966).

39. *Ibid.*

40. *Louis Riel: Poésies de jeunesse,* p. 153.

41. *Ibid.,* p. 155.

The Political Thought of Louis Riel

1. G. Martel, G. Campbell, T.E. Flanagan, *Louis Riel: Poésies de jeunesse,* (St. Boniface, 1977), pp. 149-156.

2. S. D. Clark, *The Developing Canadian Community,* (2nd ed., Toronto, 1967), pp. 207-220.

3. Flanagan, "Political Theory of the Red River Resistance: The Declaration of December 8, 1869,; *Canadian Journal of Policical Science,* 11 (March, 1978).

4. See Flanagan, "Louis 'David' Riel: Prophet, Priest-King, Infallible Pontiff," *Journal of Canadian Studies,* 9 (August, 1974), pp. 12-15; and *idem,* "Louis Riel: Insanity and Prophecy," in Howard Palmer (ed.), *The Settlement of the West* (Calgary, 1977), pp. 15-36.

5. Flanagan, "The Mission of Louis Riel." *Alberta History,* 23 (Winter, 1975), pp. 1-12.

6. A. S. Morton, "The New Nation, the Métis," *Transactions of the Royal Society of Canada,* Third Series, Section II, Vol. 33 (1939) pp. 137-145.

7. *Poésies de jeunesse,* op. cit., pp. 130-135.

8. *Ibid.,* pp. 105-108.

9. W. L. Morton, *Alexander Begg's Red River Journal,* (Toronto, 1956), p. 3.

10. "Declaration of December 8, 1869," *op.cit.,* cf. note 3, *supra.*

11. W. L. Morton, *op. cit.,* p. 137.

12. Gilles Martel, *Le Messianisme de Louis Riel (1884-1885),* (Ph.D. Thesis, Paris, Ecole des hautes études, 1976), p. 264.

13. *Ibid.,* p. 265.

14. Léon Pouliot (ed.), "Correspondance Louis Riel-Mgr Bourget," *Revue d'Histoire de l'Amérique française,* (Dec. 1961), p. 440.
15. *Journal of Canadian Studies,* op. cit., pp. 19-20. cf. note 4, supra.
16. *Ibid.,* p. 22.
17. *Ibid.* pp. 18-19.
18. For the letter, see *Le Manitoba,* June 18, 1885. The poem is in the Provincial Archives of Manitoba, Riel Family Papers (1966).
19. Alexander C. Botkin, "The John Brown of the Half Breeds, " *Rocky Mountain Magazine,* 1 (1900), p. 19.
20. Provincial Archives of Manitoba, Riel Family Papers (1966).
21. *Ibid.*
22. *Ibid.*
23. Louis Schmidt, "Mouvement des Métis à St. Laurent," March 7, 1885. Archevêché de St.-Boniface.
24. Riel, "O mon Seigneur Jésus Christ..." Archives Nationales du Québec, AP-P-1791.
25. Schmidt. *op. cit.*
26. Flanagan, (ed.), *The Diaries of Louis Riel* (Edmonton, 1976), p. 52.
27. Desmond Morton (ed.), *The Queen v. Louis Riel* (Toronto, 1974), pp. 355-56; Flanagan (ed.), "Louis Riel's Religious Beliefs: A Letter to Bishop Taché," *Saskatchewan History,* 27 (1974), pp. 15-28; Riel to J. A. Macdonald, July 6, 1885, Public Archives of Canada, Macdonald Papers; *The Diaries of Louis Riel, op. cit.,* p. 169.
28. *Winnipeg Sun,* July 3, 1885, pp. 15 ff.
29. *The Queen v Louis Riel,* p. 319.
30. Riel to Macdonald, July 6, 1885, *op. cit.,* and July 16, 1885, Public Archives of Canada, Ministry of Justice, Records Relating to Louis Riel and the North West Uprising.
31. Riel to Cleveland, n.d. National Archives of the United States, Consular despatches from Winnipeg, Department of State Records.
32. *Diaries,* p. 166.
33. *Saskatchewan History, op. cit. cf.* note 27, *supra.*
34. *Cf.* a poem, "Dans l'état du Minnesota," in P.A.M., Riel Family Papers (1966).
35. Lewis H. Thomas, "Louis Riel's Petition of Rights, 1884," *Saskatchewan History,* 23 (Winter, 1970), p. 19. The title of this article is rather misleading. The petition was as much Jackson's work as Riel's. Riel did not sign it, nor did it represent his real thinking.
36. *Cf.* the "Lists of Rights" in W. L. Morton, (ed.), *Manitoba: The Birth of a Province* (Altona, Manitoba, 1965), pp. 242-250.
37. Section 31 of the Manitoba Act, *ibid.,* p. 258.
38. On the land grant and its aftermath, see M. Giraud, *Le Métis canadien* (Paris, 1945), Vol. II, pp. 1116-1124; A. S. Morton, *History of Prairie*

    Settlement (Toronto, 1938), pp. 48-49, Chester Martin, *"Dominion Lands" Policy,* (Toronto, 1938), pp. 236-239.

39. National Archives of the United States, Records of the Adjutant General's Office. Petition dated August 6, 1880.

40. Reproduced in Schmidt, op. cit. Cf. note 23, *supra.*

41. Martel, *op. cit.,* pp. 379-406.

42. Thomas, *op. cit. Cf.* note 35 supra.

43. E. G. Peter Charlebois, *The Life of Louis Riel,* (Toronto, 1975).

44. "Declaration of December 8, 1869," *op. cit. Cf* note 3, *supra.*

45. Cited in Mason Wade, *The French Canadians 1760-1967,* (2nd ed., Toronto, 1968), p. 360.

46. Archives of the Seminary of Quebec, Riel Papers, p. 88.

47. *Cf.* G. F. G. Stanley, *Louis Riel,* (Toronto, 1963), p. 223.

48. Riel to Taché, n.d. but *ca.* 1877. Archives of the Seminary of Trois-Rivières.

49. T. E. Flanagan (ed.), "The Riel 'Lunacy Commission': The Report of Dr. Valade," *Revue de l'Université d'Ottawa,* 46 (1976), p. 122.

50. Riel, n.d. but *ca.* August-November, 1885. Archevêché de St.-Boniface.